KING

1

Written & Illustrated
BY HO CHE ANDERSON

1993...

...Which makes it 25 years since the Reverend Doctor Martin Luther King was murdered on a hotel balcony in Memphis, Tennessee. It's been 25 years since the civil rights struggle was daily, front-page news, an omnipresent concern of the nation; 25 years since "official," nationwide *integration* took hold, supposedly the beginning of the answer to all of our problems. But I find I'm forced to ask myself what has changed. I say none of this by way of criticizing Whites; as far as I'm concerned, the days of blaming the White man for the problems in our own home are over and done with. But let's just examine this for a moment because I'm a young man; and I need someone to answer my questions. With the advent of integration, Black people have ceased to be entrepreneurs on the scale they once were. We are now less likely to patronize one of our own stores than one owned by White people, contributing to the breakdown in the economy of our communities. Partly as a result of *that,* Black children are among the worst educated, the most likely to be seduced by crime, the most likely to be murdered. And any Blacks who want to criticize me for saying that, go right ahead. I ain't making this shit up. *Children* are taking guns and knives to schools! *Children* are being murdered over pairs of sneakers or for mistakenly walking through the wrong neighborhood. Is it just me, or does it seem like vocal, visible hate groups are on the rise? When I read the papers or watch the news I see far too much of this. Is it just a case of the media trying to start some shit, or do we have to examine those things before they get worse? Better the enemy you can see than the one you cannot. But now it's 1993. Twenty-five years later, we were supposed to be beyond this madness.

• • •

I was offered the opportunity to do this book in the spring of 1990, to tell the story of one of the 20th Century's great leaders as my conscience guided me. If I said my intentions at the time were pure and righteous, I'd be lying to your face — I needed a job, and this looked like a great gig. You have to understand where I've come from. In my younger years, I was an assimilation junkie — without even realizing it — trying to fit into White society by any means necessary. I wish I could say this was uncommon, but I can't. Like so many young Blacks, my eyes were so closed to myself as a people, I was effectively blind. I thought I knew what my shit was about. Martin King was never a big hero of mine; his life and struggles were the farthest things from my mind.

It's difficult to say exactly where the changes occurred, at what points along the road I became self-aware, when who I was began to matter to me, when telling the stories of Black people became one of the most important things in my life...

KING did not instigate those changes; I was already well on the way when this project was first proposed. But this has gone beyond a good gig; it's become a story I *have* to tell. Originally, KING was planned to be three small, stapled comics totaling no more than 90 pages of story and art. Ninety pages to tell the story of one of the great men of our times. But as it approached the green-light stage, *I knew,* I think I always knew, that it had to be *big.* You can't tell a story as important as this in a truncated, *Reader's Digest* version. You cannot do it. I had to tell it right, or not at all. And so, on March 2 of '92, after six dizzying months of research, I began working on my script and completed it three months later on June 4, just after the L.A. riots/uprising. It came in at a cool 150 pages, lean and mean, my interpretation of the man, Martin Luther King. Not the media-created demigod among mortals, not the superhuman orator with the Dream, but the man, no bullshit, no hype, straight, no chaser.

In doing the research for this comic book, I read two biographies, and various books on and about the times, watched nearly 35 hours of documentary footage, and studied newspaper articles and photos of the period. Had the option to interview the real-life players in the saga been open to me, I would surely have availed myself. Above and beyond the research done, I want to stress that this is my *interpretation* of the man. KING is by *no means* definitive; it is *one* voice among *many.* It was necessary to take *some* dramatic license. For example, only two people know for sure what was said between JFK and MLK in their Rose Garden meetings — and they're both dead. Furthermore, I am not a mouthpiece for the King legacy. Mine is not an uncritical eye. This ain't a collection of "King's greatest hits." I've tried to present a well-rounded portrait: some of the flaws and some of the triumphs, tempered by the tremendous respect I've discovered within myself for Martin King. That respect is on every page of this volume. This is the picture *I* saw.

In my heart, I'm an optimist. I'd like to think that Black people are starting to grow up. I do see signs, but I don't know. I am certainly *not* the voice of Black rage in comics; it's not a mantle I want. I'm just asking questions and hoping for some answers — like the rest of us. But it has been *25 years.* As Black people, we're *still* waiting for this so-called "promised land." And I have to wonder, sometimes: does the damned thing even exist?

Nineteen-ninety-three, and counting...

Ho Che Anderson
5/28/93

He was driving by in a limousine. In a black limousine.... Big, black...block-long thing. I remember that he was a very good-looking young man.

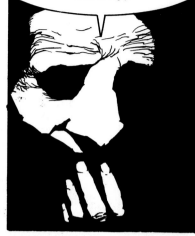

Too young for me but very pretty... The memory fades after a certain age, but I do remember that he was a very handsome young man.

I'm from the South, the grand ol' traditions that are the South. At the time us Southern niggers looked on him as a trouble-maker. Too much trouble made them White devil mothers angry.

I'm going to speak to you in the modern vernacular. King pissed-me-off. *Ha, ha*... Heh, heh, heh.... Yeah, boy, the way he was around women, so smooth, so very smooth. Damn....

THE

ATTESTORS

One time my wife and I who was my *"piece"* at the time, my ladyfriend, went to listen to the man speak at a student rally and after just a minute or two of listening to that seductive baritone rumble of his, Francine was under his spell.

The girl was in deep! Forgot *all about* me. She would have fallen at his feet in love with him had he asked. Good Lord! He *was* nice, but I wanted him put to sleep or lynched. Seriously, he *was* a good man....

I suppose I can look back on things from that period with objective eyes now. You know how it's difficult sometimes to admit things about yourself at the time.... That was me *then* so it doesn't affect me now. Maybe I *was* an Uncle Tom.... I have a successful business now. A nice house for the family. Maybe some of that I owe to Martin King.

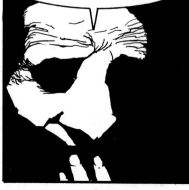

Well, no, no, no, I don't. I don't talk about him, no. We were not friends. I assume you want me to say something *nice* about him...well, I *have* nothing nice to say about him. When you asked me to be a part of this I *told* you I had nothing nice to say about him.

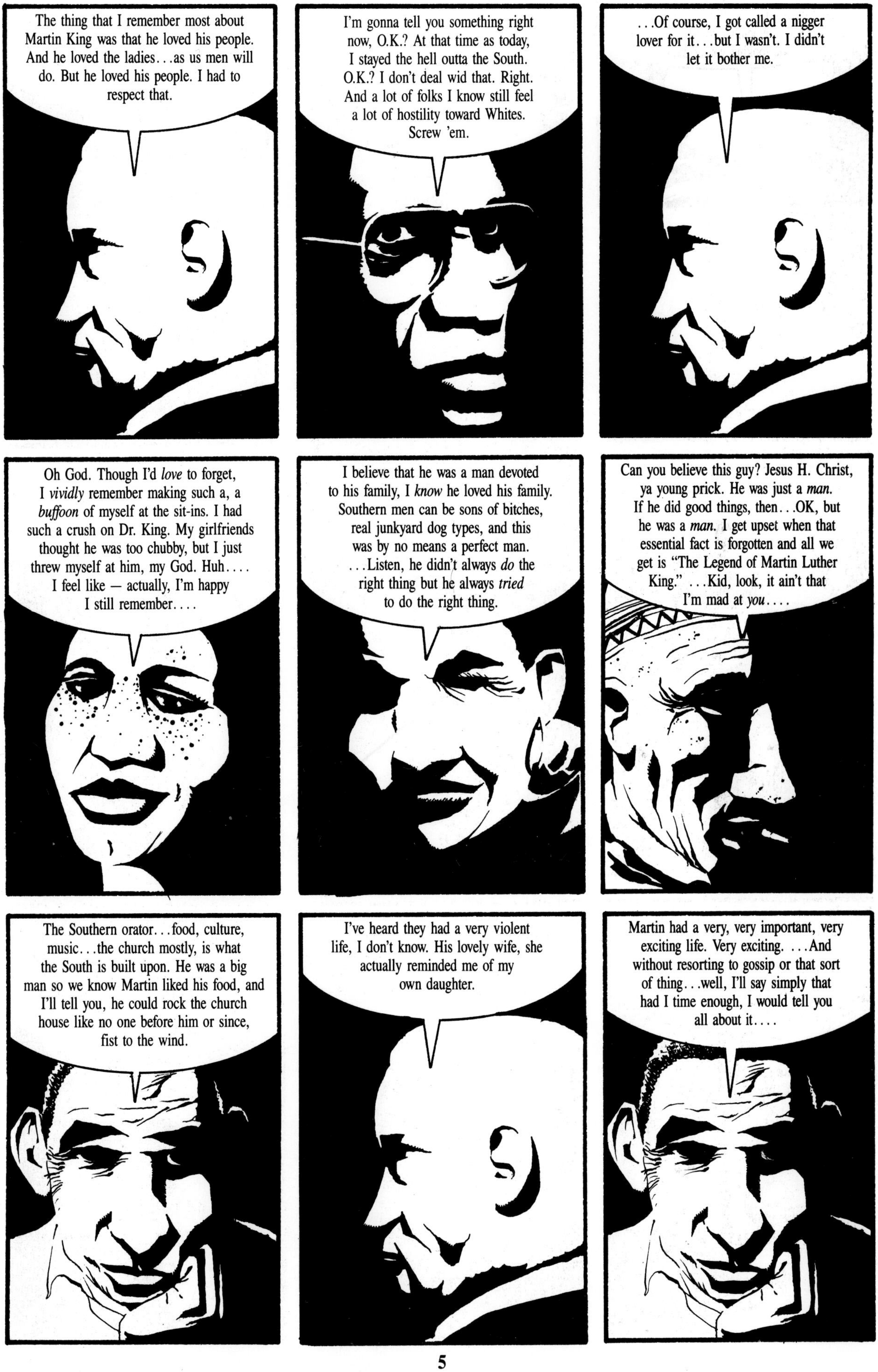
The thing that I remember most about Martin King was that he loved his people. And he loved the ladies...as us men will do. But he loved his people. I had to respect that.
I'm gonna tell you something right now, O.K.? At that time as today, I stayed the hell outta the South. O.K.? I don't deal wid that. Right. And a lot of folks I know still feel a lot of hostility toward Whites. Screw 'em.
...Of course, I got called a nigger lover for it...but I wasn't. I didn't let it bother me.
Oh God. Though I'd *love* to forget, I *vividly* remember making such a, a *buffoon* of myself at the sit-ins. I had such a crush on Dr. King. My girlfriends thought he was too chubby, but I just threw myself at him, my God. Huh.... I feel like — actually, I'm happy I still remember....
I believe that he was a man devoted to his family, I *know* he loved his family. Southern men can be sons of bitches, real junkyard dog types, and this was by no means a perfect man. ...Listen, he didn't always *do* the right thing but he always *tried* to do the right thing.
Can you believe this guy? Jesus H. Christ, ya young prick. He was just a *man*. If he did good things, then...OK, but he was a *man*. I get upset when that essential fact is forgotten and all we get is "The Legend of Martin Luther King." ...Kid, look, it ain't that I'm mad at *you*....
The Southern orator...food, culture, music...the church mostly, is what the South is built upon. He was a big man so we know Martin liked his food, and I'll tell you, he could rock the church house like no one before him or since, fist to the wind.
I've heard they had a very violent life, I don't know. His lovely wife, she actually reminded me of my own daughter.
Martin had a very, very important, very exciting life. Very exciting. ...And without resorting to gossip or that sort of thing...well, I'll say simply that had I time enough, I would tell you all about it....

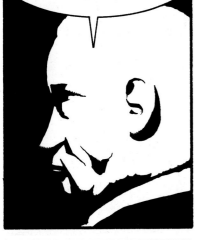

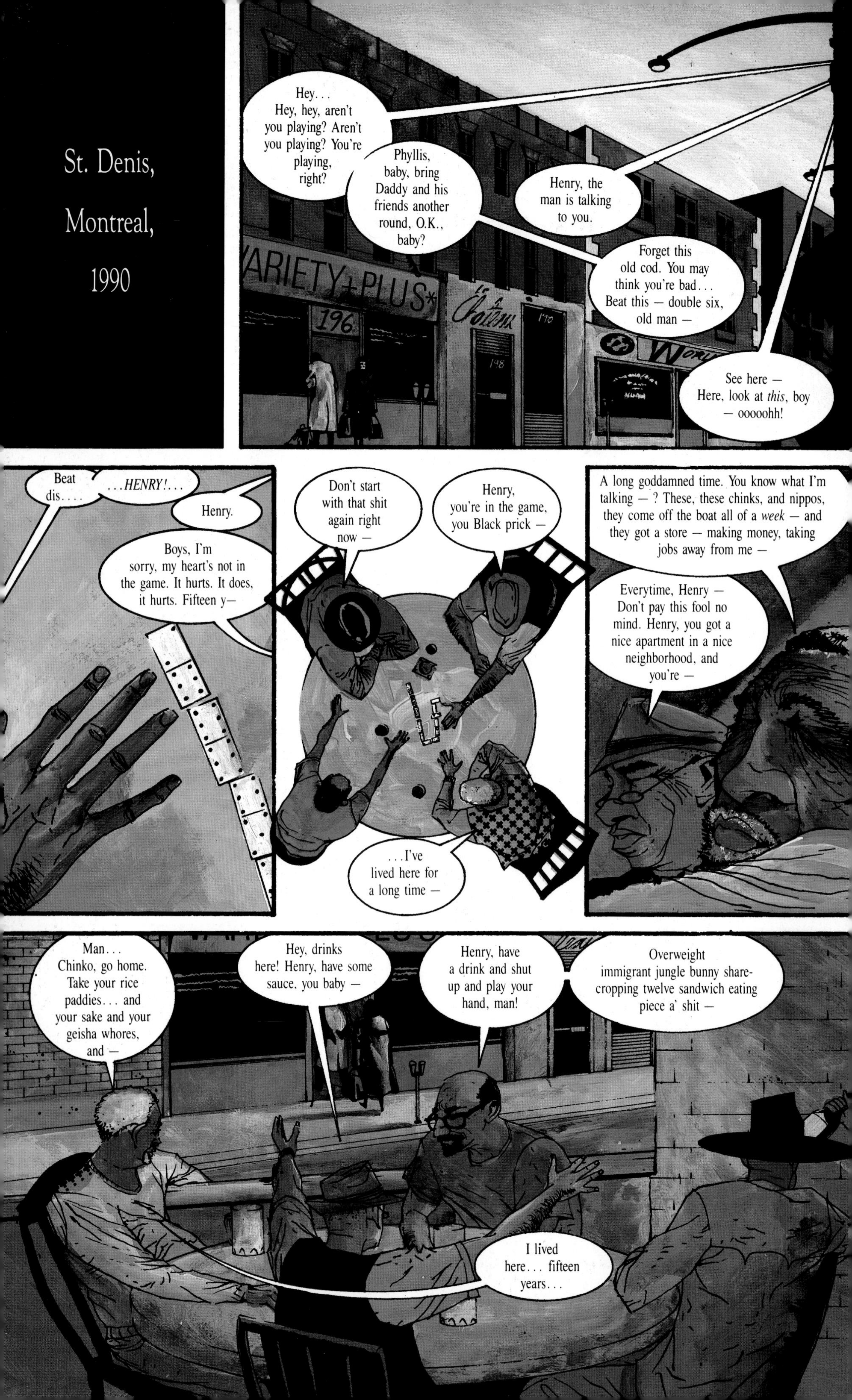
St. Denis, Montreal, 1990
Hey... Hey, hey, aren't you playing? Aren't you playing? You're playing, right?
Phyllis, baby, bring Daddy and his friends another round, O.K., baby?
Henry, the man is talking to you.
Forget this old cod. You may think you're bad... Beat this — double six, old man —
See here — Here, look at *this*, boy — oooohh!
Beat dis....
...*HENRY!*...
Henry.
Boys, I'm sorry, my heart's not in the game. It hurts. It does, it hurts. Fifteen y—
Don't start with that shit again right now —
Henry, you're in the game, you Black prick —
...I've lived here for a long time —
A long goddamned time. You know what I'm talking — ? These, these chinks, and nippos, they come off the boat all of a *week* — and they got a store — making money, taking jobs away from me —
Everytime, Henry — Don't pay this fool no mind. Henry, you got a nice apartment in a nice neighborhood, and you're —
Man... Chinko, go home. Take your rice paddies... and your sake and your geisha whores, and —
Hey, drinks here! Henry, have some sauce, you baby —
Henry, have a drink and shut up and play your hand, man!
Overweight immigrant jungle bunny share-cropping twelve sandwich eating piece a' shit —
I lived here... fifteen years...

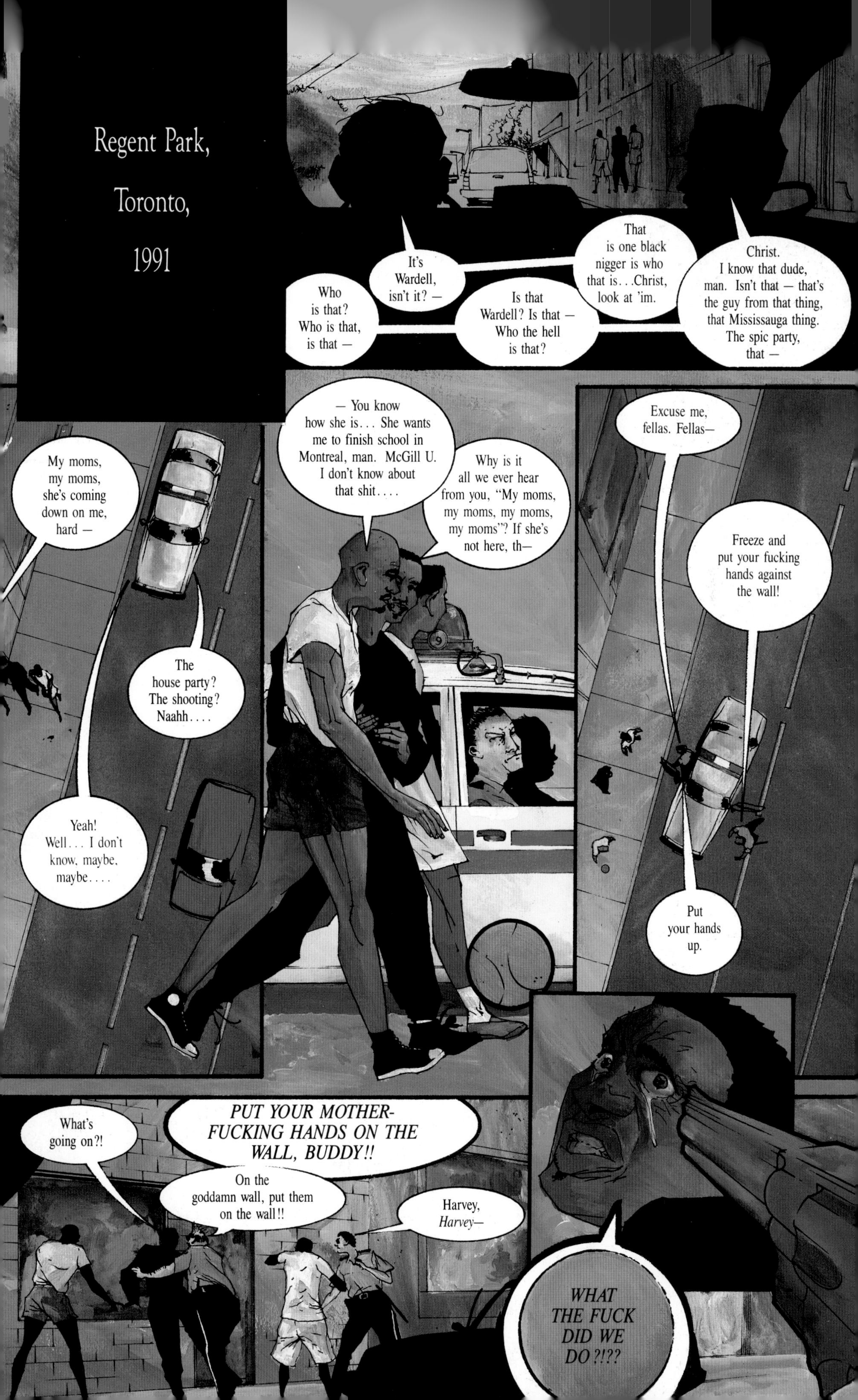
Regent Park, Toronto, 1991
Who is that? Who is that, is that —
It's Wardell, isn't it? —
Is that Wardell? Is that — Who the hell is that?
That is one black nigger is who that is. . .Christ, look at 'im.
Christ. I know that dude, man. Isn't that — that's the guy from that thing, that Mississauga thing. The spic party, that —
My moms, my moms, she's coming down on me, hard —
The house party? The shooting? Naahh. . . .
Yeah! Well. . . I don't know, maybe, maybe. . . .
— You know how she is. . . She wants me to finish school in Montreal, man. McGill U. I don't know about that shit. . . .
Why is it all we ever hear from you, "My moms, my moms, my moms, my moms"? If she's not here, th—
Excuse me, fellas. Fellas—
Freeze and put your fucking hands against the wall!
Put your hands up.
What's going on?!
PUT YOUR MOTHER-FUCKING HANDS ON THE WALL, BUDDY!!
On the goddamn wall, put them on the wall!!
Harvey, *Harvey*—
WHAT THE FUCK DID WE DO?!??

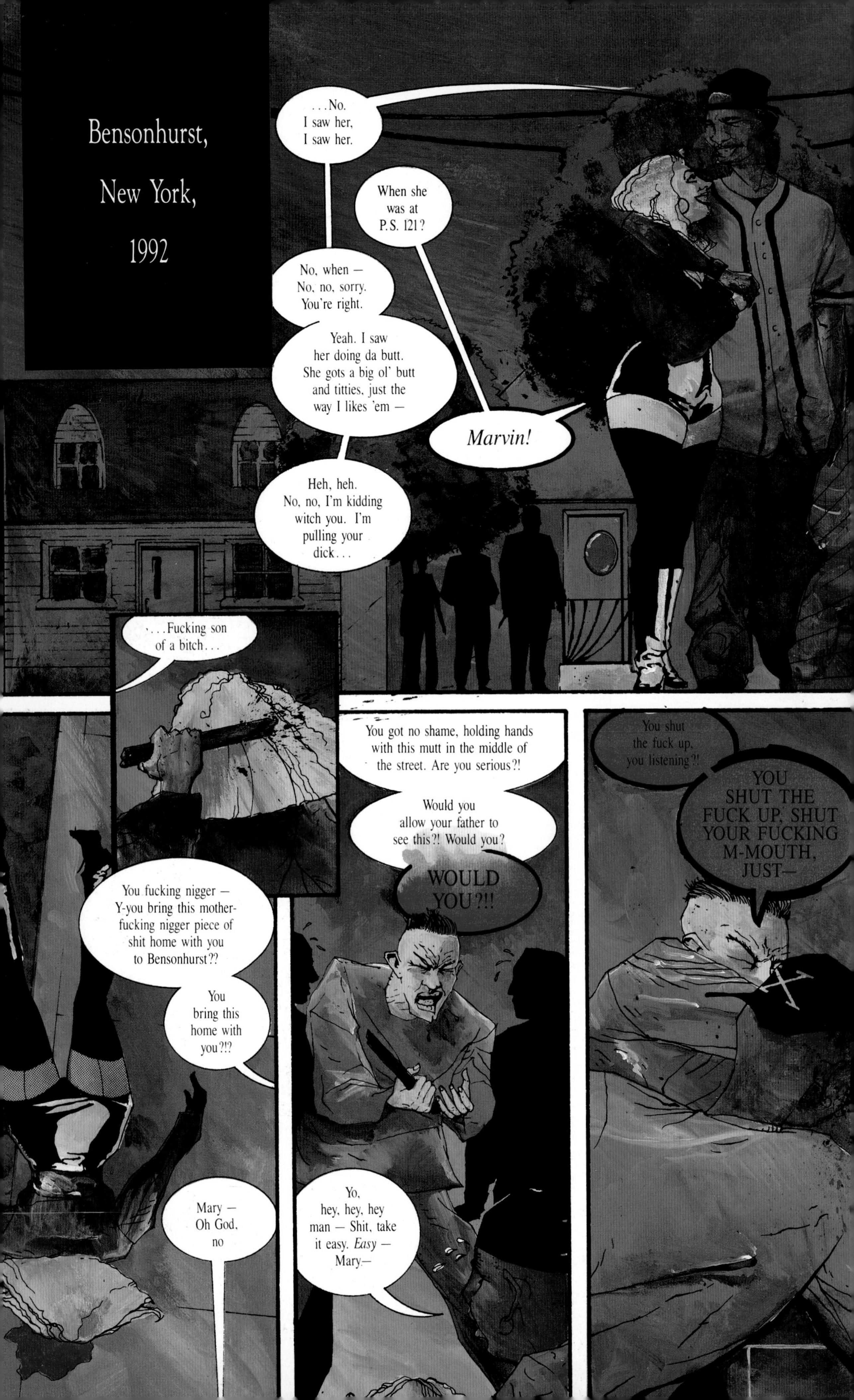
Bensonhurst, New York, 1992
...No. I saw her, I saw her.
When she was at P.S. 121?
No, when — No, no, sorry. You're right.
Yeah. I saw her doing da butt. She gots a big ol' butt and titties, just the way I likes 'em —
Marvin!
Heh, heh. No, no, I'm kidding witch you. I'm pulling your dick...
...Fucking son of a bitch...
You fucking nigger — Y-you bring this mother-fucking nigger piece of shit home with you to Bensonhurst??
You bring this home with you?!?
Mary — Oh God, no
You got no shame, holding hands with this mutt in the middle of the street. Are you serious?!
Would you allow your father to see this?! Would you?
WOULD YOU?!!
Yo, hey, hey, hey man — Shit, take it easy. Easy — Mary.—
You shut the fuck up, you listening?!
YOU SHUT THE FUCK UP, SHUT YOUR FUCKING M-MOUTH, JUST—

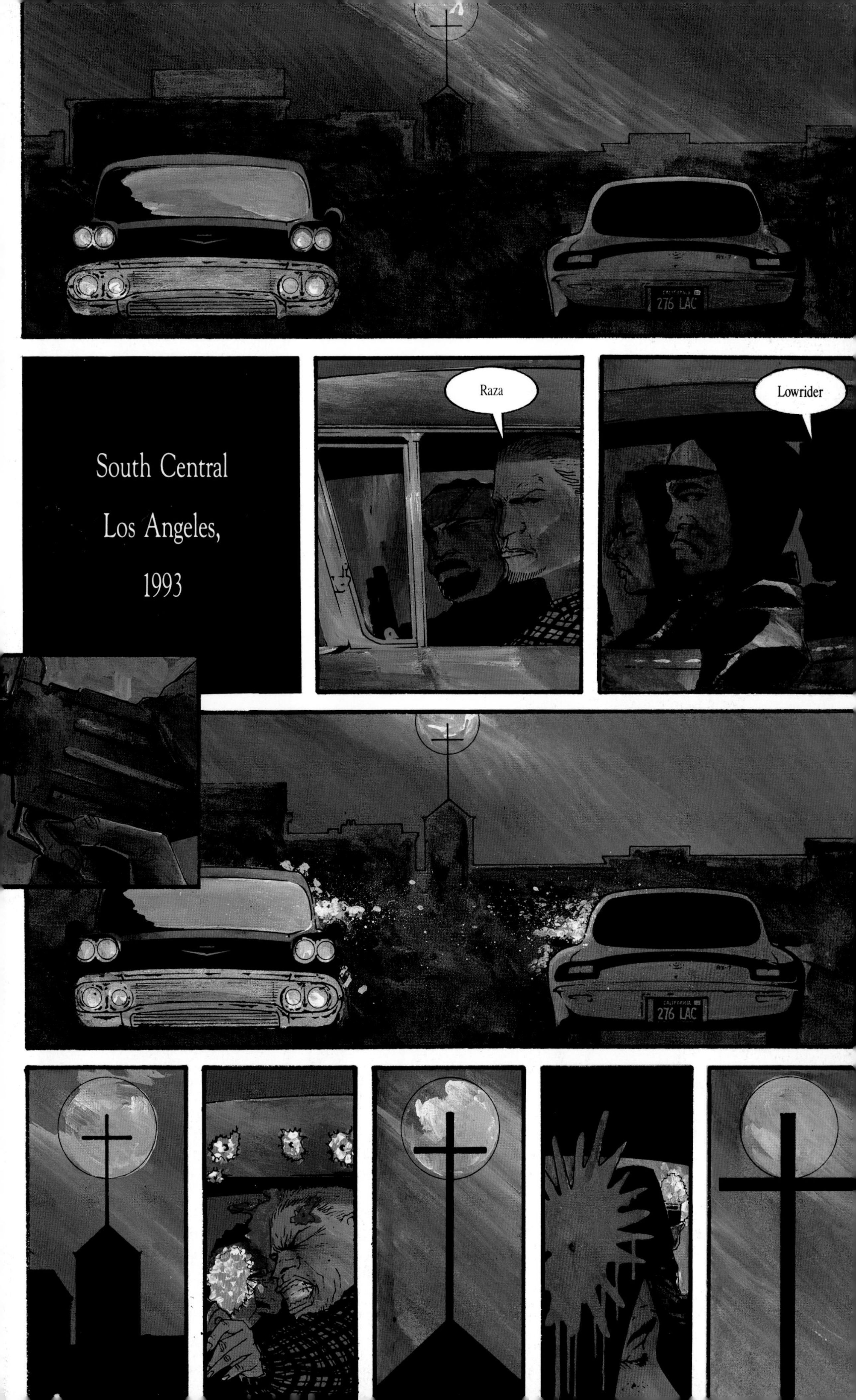
CALIFORNIA
276 LAC
South Central
Los Angeles,
1993
Raza
Lowrider
CALIFORNIA
276 LAC

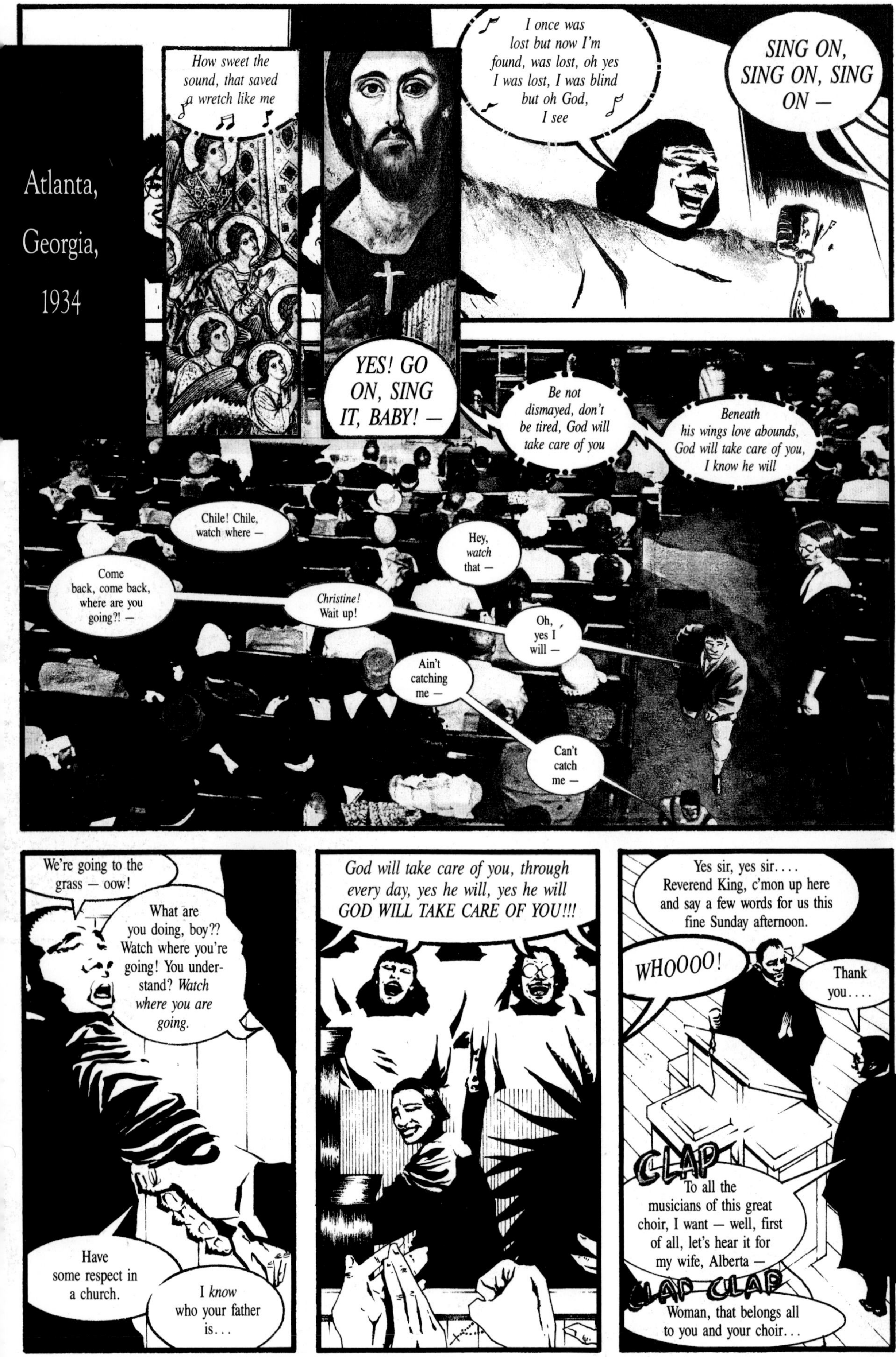
Atlanta, Georgia, 1934
How sweet the sound, that saved a wretch like me
I once was lost but now I'm found, was lost, oh yes I was lost, I was blind but oh God, I see
SING ON, SING ON, SING ON —
YES! GO ON, SING IT, BABY! —
Be not dismayed, don't be tired, God will take care of you
Beneath his wings love abounds, God will take care of you, I know he will
Chile! Chile, watch where —
Hey, watch that —
Come back, come back, where are you going?! —
Christine! Wait up!
Oh, yes I will —
Ain't catching me —
Can't catch me —
We're going to the grass — oow!
What are you doing, boy?? Watch where you're going! You understand? Watch where you are going.
Have some respect in a church.
I know who your father is...
God will take care of you, through every day, yes he will, yes he will GOD WILL TAKE CARE OF YOU!!!
Yes sir, yes sir.... Reverend King, c'mon up here and say a few words for us this fine Sunday afternoon.
WHOOOO!
Thank you....
CLAP
To all the musicians of this great choir, I want — well, first of all, let's hear it for my wife, Alberta —
CLAP CLAP
Woman, that belongs all to you and your choir...

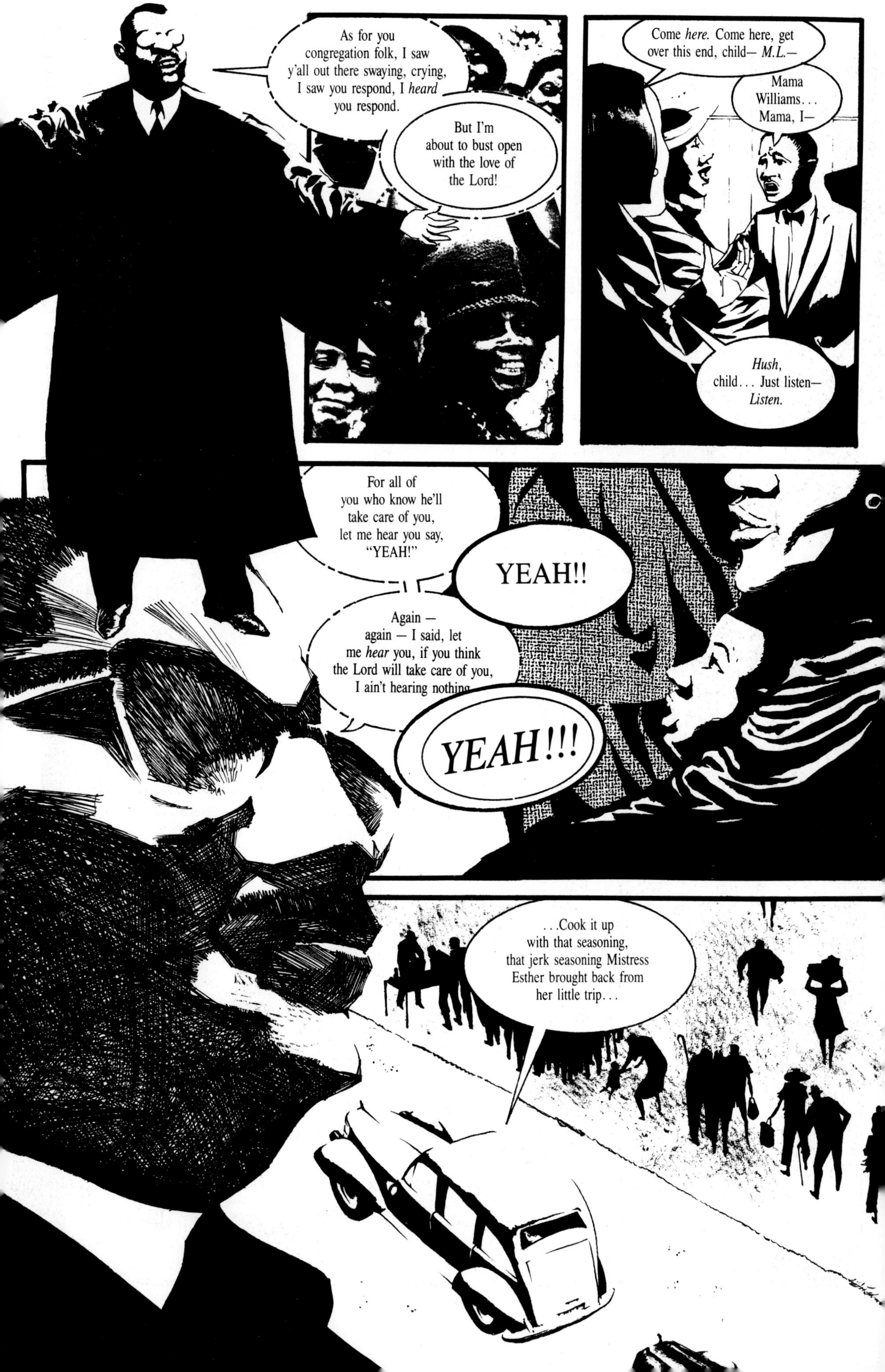

As for you congregation folk, I saw y'all out there swaying, crying, I saw you respond, I *heard* you respond.
But I'm about to bust open with the love of the Lord!
Come *here.* Come here, get over this end, child— *M.L.*—
Mama Williams... Mama, I—
Hush, child... Just listen— *Listen.*
For all of you who know he'll take care of you, let me hear you say, "YEAH!"
YEAH!!
Again — again — I said, let me *hear* you, if you think the Lord will take care of you, I ain't hearing nothing
YEAH!!!
...Cook it up with that seasoning, that jerk seasoning Mistress Esther brought back from her little trip...

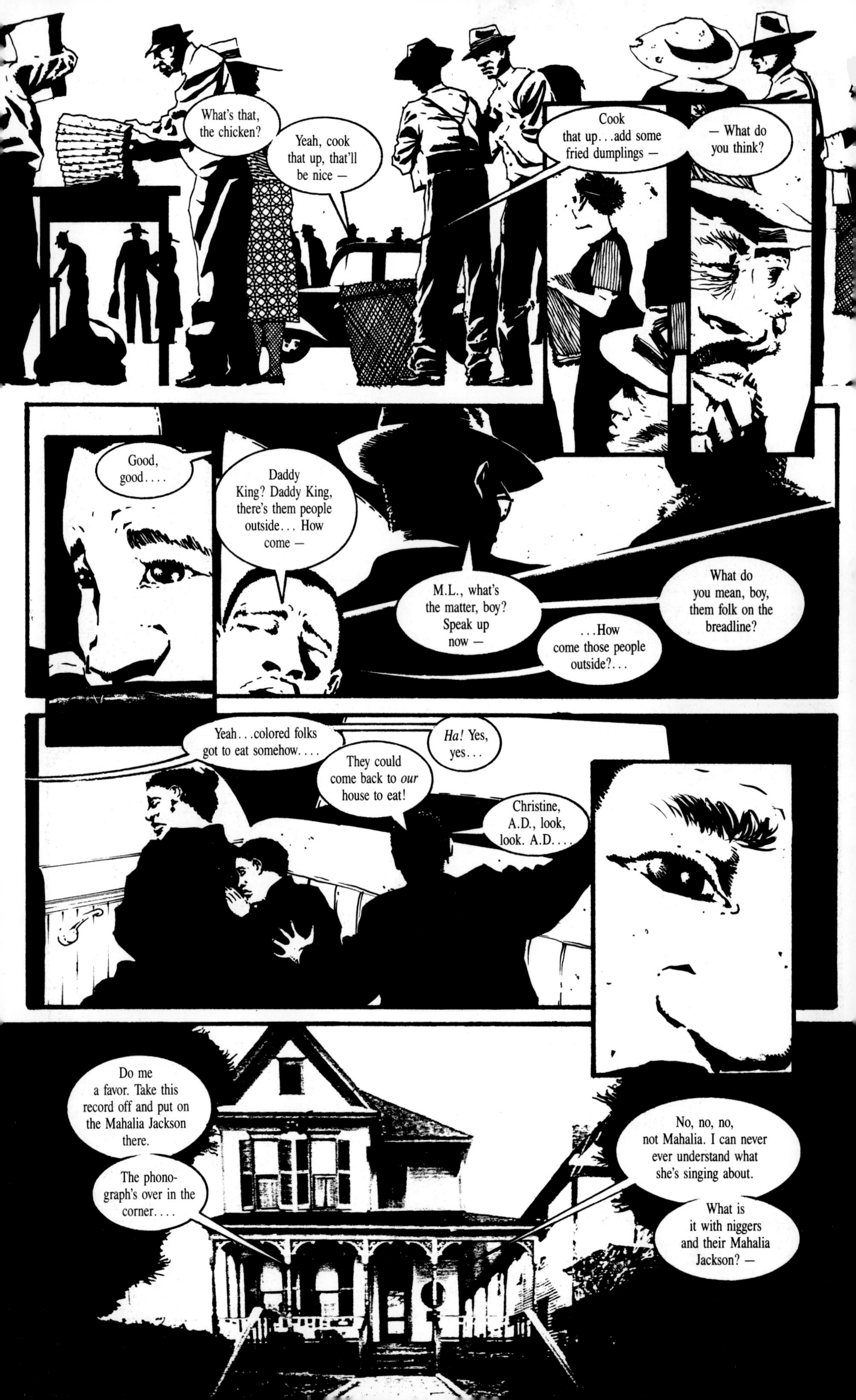
What's that, the chicken?
Yeah, cook that up, that'll be nice –
Cook that up...add some fried dumplings –
– What do you think?
Good, good....
Daddy King? Daddy King, there's them people outside... How come –
M.L., what's the matter, boy? Speak up now –
...How come those people outside?...
What do you mean, boy, them folk on the breadline?
Yeah...colored folks got to eat somehow....
They could come back to *our* house to eat!
Ha! Yes, yes...
Christine, A.D., look, look. A.D....
Do me a favor. Take this record off and put on the Mahalia Jackson there.
The phonograph's over in the corner....
No, no, no, not Mahalia. I can never ever understand what she's singing about.
What is it with niggers and their Mahalia Jackson? –

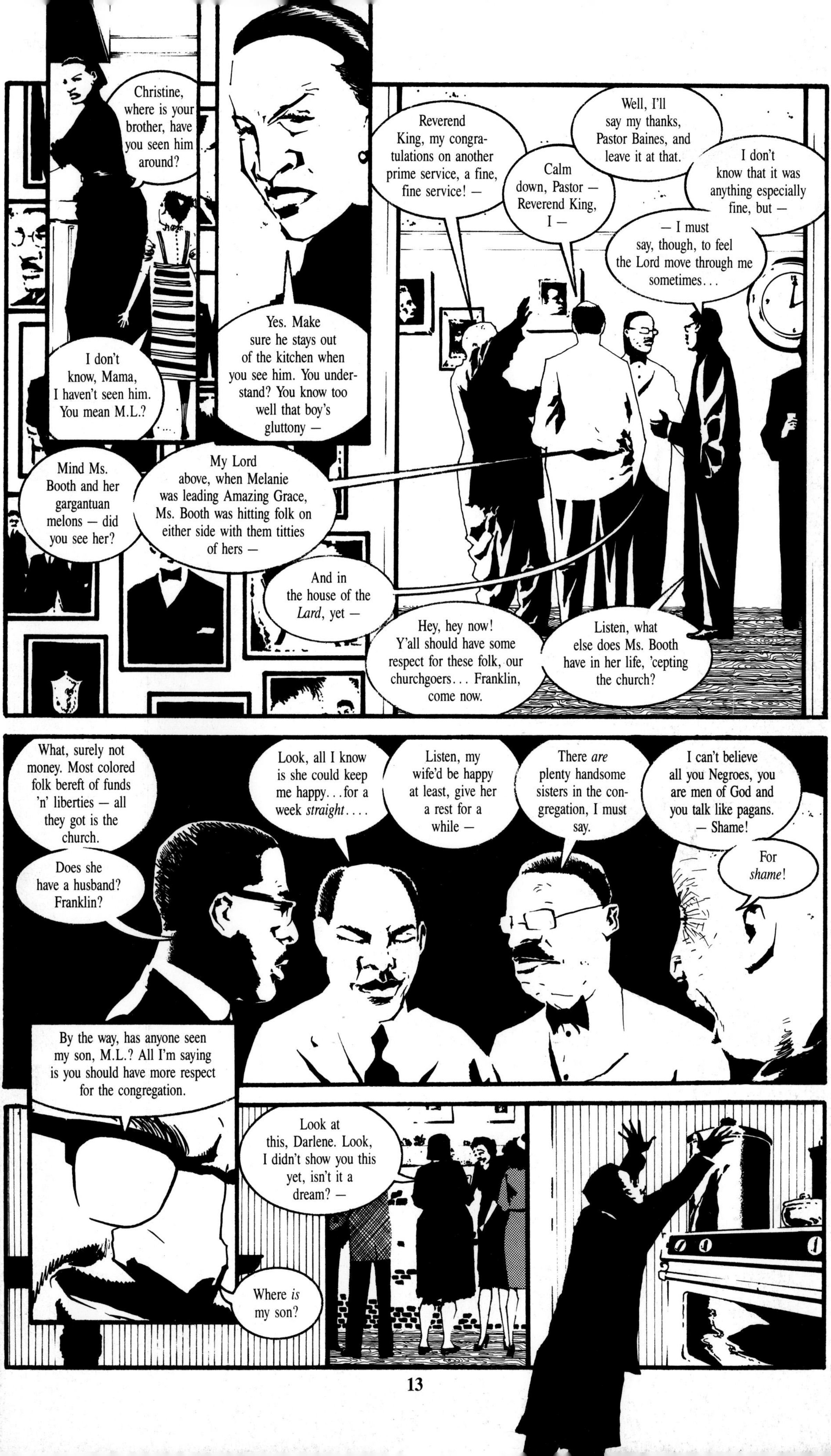
Christine, where is your brother, have you seen him around?
I don't know, Mama, I haven't seen him. You mean M.L.?
Yes. Make sure he stays out of the kitchen when you see him. You understand? You know too well that boy's gluttony —
Reverend King, my congratulations on another prime service, a fine, fine service! —
Calm down, Pastor — Reverend King, I —
Well, I'll say my thanks, Pastor Baines, and leave it at that.
I don't know that it was anything especially fine, but —
— I must say, though, to feel the Lord move through me sometimes...
Mind Ms. Booth and her gargantuan melons — did you see her?
My Lord above, when Melanie was leading Amazing Grace, Ms. Booth was hitting folk on either side with them titties of hers —
And in the house of the *Lard*, yet —
Hey, hey now! Y'all should have some respect for these folk, our churchgoers... Franklin, come now.
Listen, what else does Ms. Booth have in her life, 'cepting the church?
What, surely not money. Most colored folk bereft of funds 'n' liberties — all they got is the church.
Does she have a husband? Franklin?
Look, all I know is she could keep me happy...for a week *straight*....
Listen, my wife'd be happy at least, give her a rest for a while —
There *are* plenty handsome sisters in the congregation, I must say.
I can't believe all you Negroes, you are men of God and you talk like pagans. — Shame!
For *shame*!
By the way, has anyone seen my son, M.L.? All I'm saying is you should have more respect for the congregation.
Where *is* my son?
Look at this, Darlene. Look, I didn't show you this yet, isn't it a dream? —

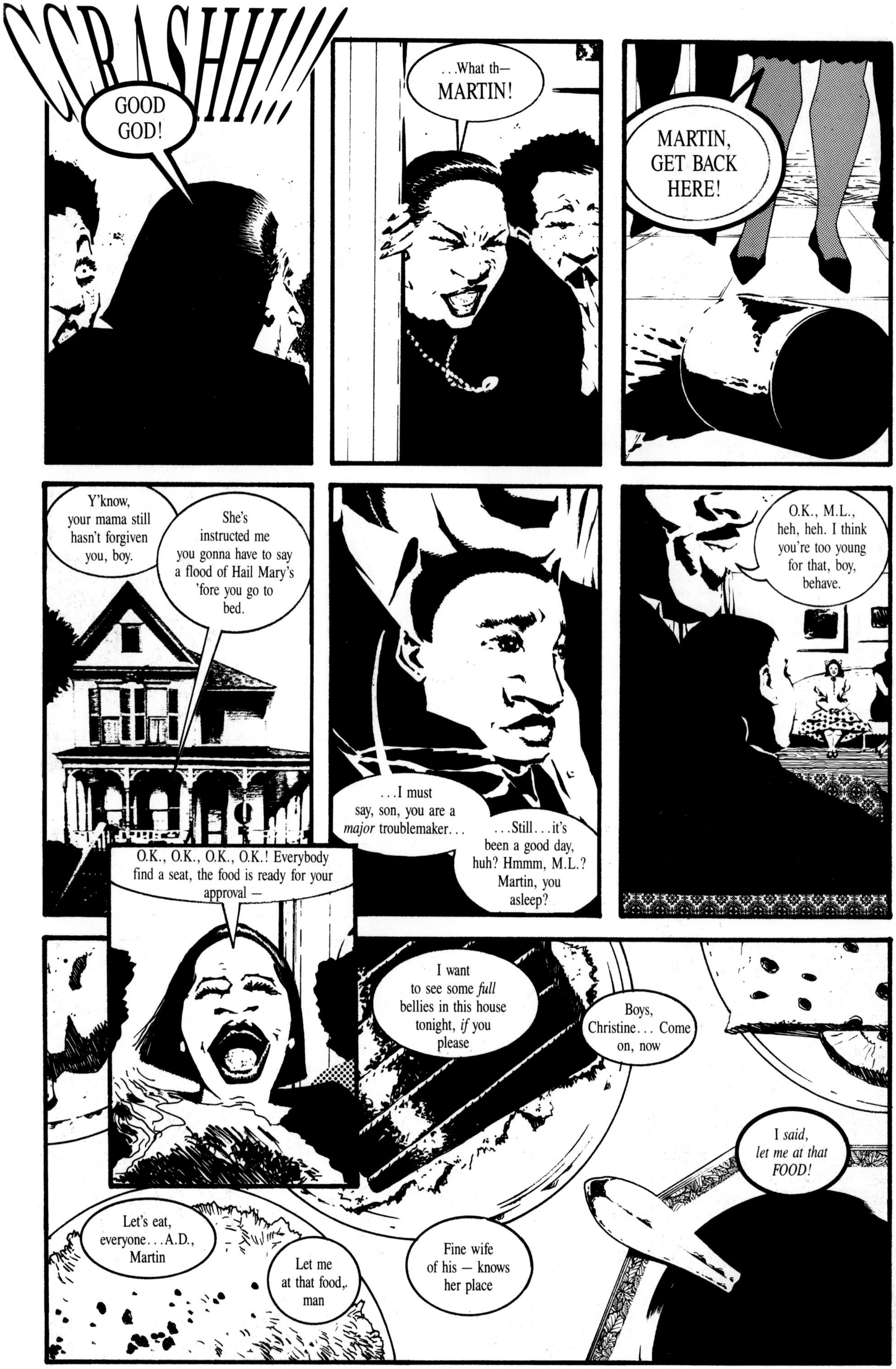
CCRASHH!!!
GOOD GOD!
. . .What th— MARTIN!
MARTIN, GET BACK HERE!
Y'know, your mama still hasn't forgiven you, boy.
She's instructed me you gonna have to say a flood of Hail Mary's 'fore you go to bed.
. . .I must say, son, you are a *major* troublemaker. . .
. . .Still. . .it's been a good day, huh? Hmmm, M.L.? Martin, you asleep?
O.K., M.L., heh, heh. I think you're too young for that, boy, behave.
O.K., O.K., O.K., O.K.! Everybody find a seat, the food is ready for your approval —
I want to see some *full* bellies in this house tonight, *if* you please
Boys, Christine. . . Come on, now
I *said*, let me at that FOOD!
Let's eat, everyone. . .A.D., Martin
Let me at that food, man
Fine wife of his — knows her place

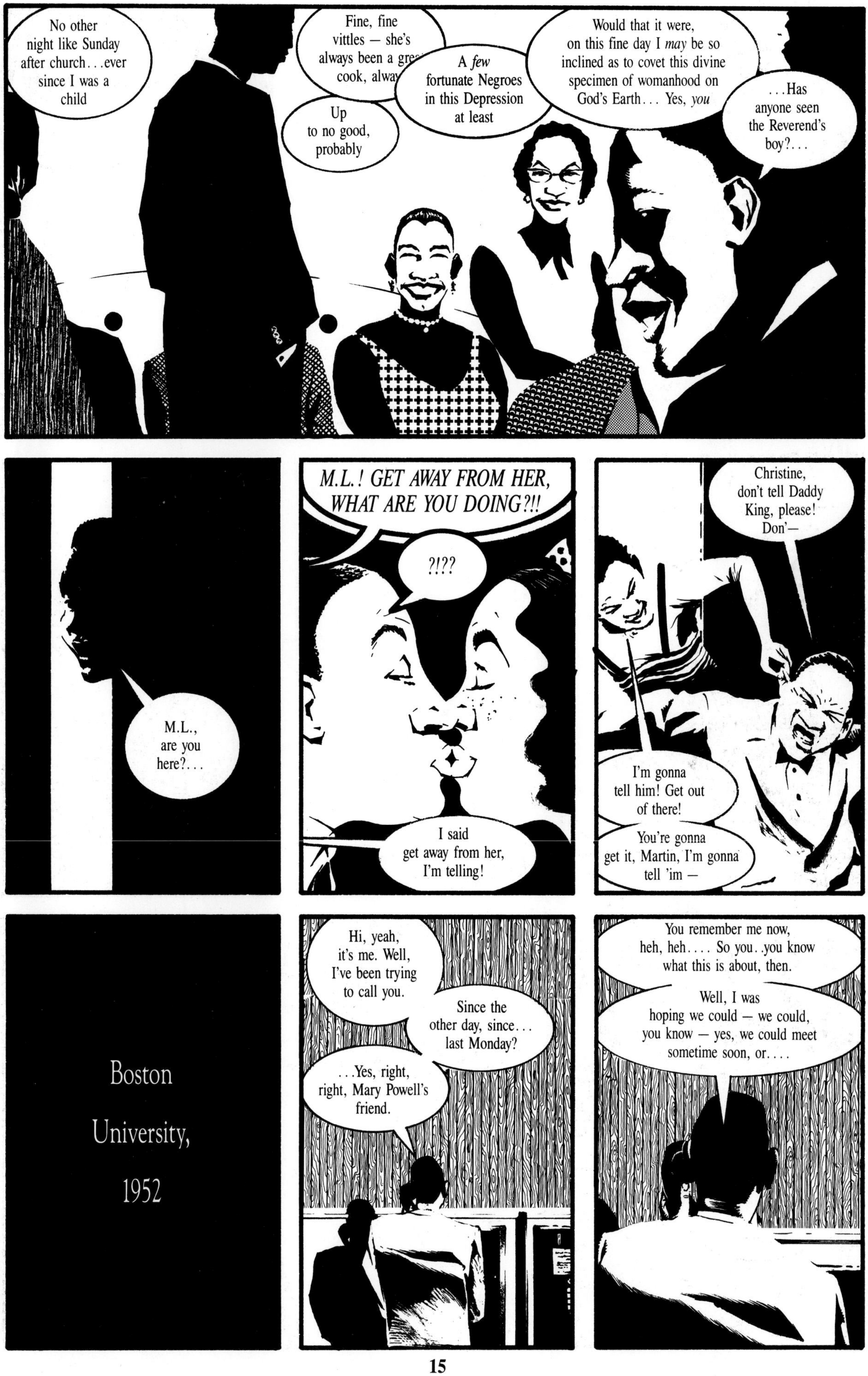

No other night like Sunday after church. . .ever since I was a child
Fine, fine vittles — she's always been a gre cook, alway
Up to no good, probably
A *few* fortunate Negroes in this Depression at least
Would that it were, on this fine day I *may* be so inclined as to covet this divine specimen of womanhood on God's Earth. . . Yes, *you*
. . .Has anyone seen the Reverend's boy?. . .
M.L., are you here?. . .
M.L.! GET AWAY FROM HER, WHAT ARE YOU DOING?!!
?!??
I said get away from her, I'm telling!
Christine, don't tell Daddy King, please! Don'—
I'm gonna tell him! Get out of there!
You're gonna get it, Martin, I'm gonna tell 'im —
Boston University, 1952
Hi, yeah, it's me. Well, I've been trying to call you.
Since the other day, since. . . last Monday?
. . .Yes, right, right, Mary Powell's friend.
You remember me now, heh, heh. . . . So you. .you know what this is about, then.
Well, I was hoping we could — we could, you know — yes, we could meet sometime soon, or. . . .

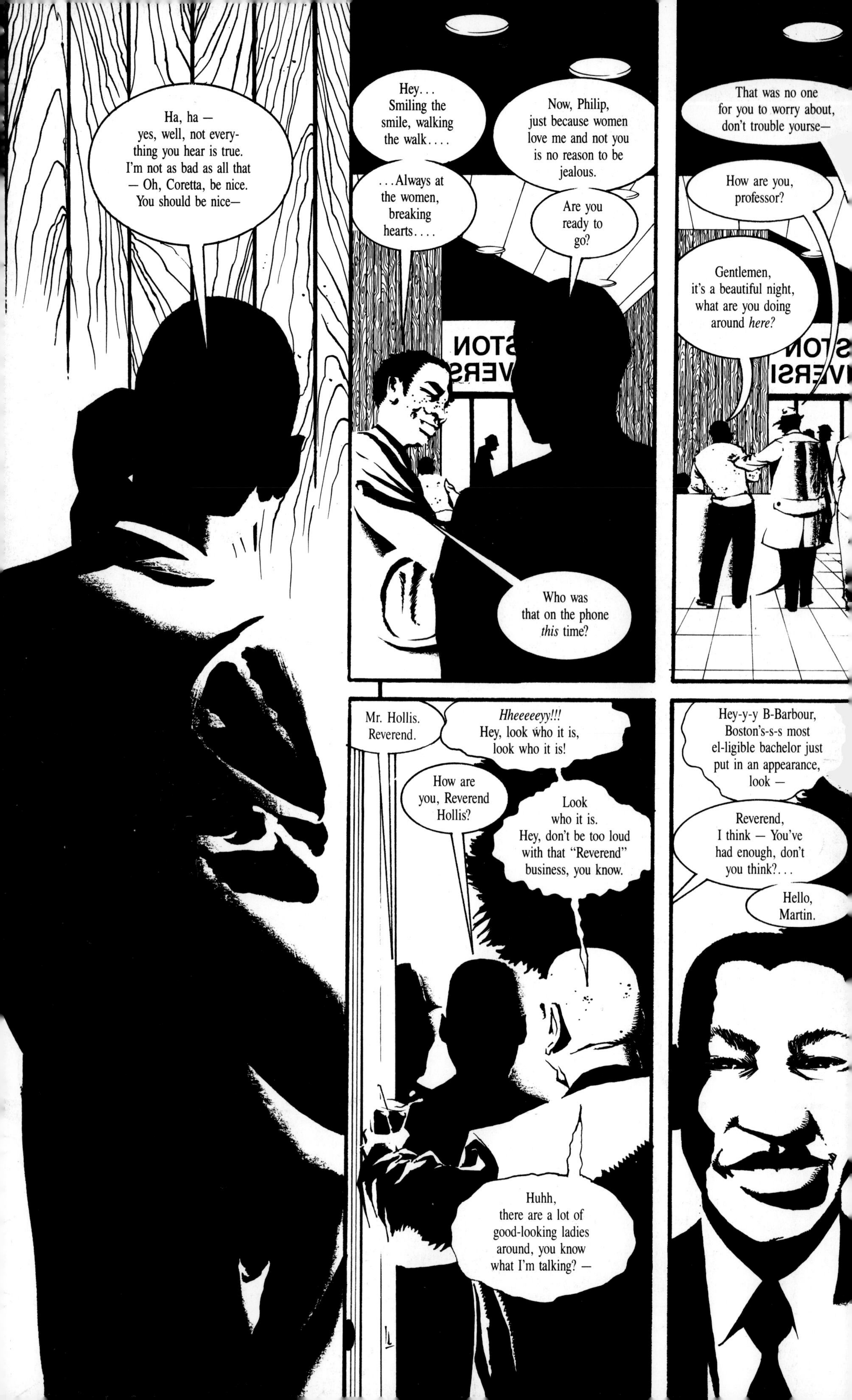
Ha, ha — yes, well, not every-thing you hear is true. I'm not as bad as all that — Oh, Coretta, be nice. You should be nice—
Hey... Smiling the smile, walking the walk....
...Always at the women, breaking hearts....
Now, Philip, just because women love me and not you is no reason to be jealous.
Are you ready to go?
Who was that on the phone *this* time?
STON
VERSI
That was no one for you to worry about, don't trouble yourse—
How are you, professor?
Gentlemen, it's a beautiful night, what are you doing around *here?*
STON
IVERSI
Mr. Hollis. Reverend.
Hheeeeeyy!!! Hey, look who it is, look who it is!
How are you, Reverend Hollis?
Look who it is. Hey, don't be too loud with that "Reverend" business, you know.
Huhh, there are a lot of good-looking ladies around, you know what I'm talking? —
Hey-y-y B-Barbour, Boston's-s-s most el-ligible bachelor just put in an appearance, look —
Reverend, I think — You've had enough, don't you think?...
Hello, Martin.

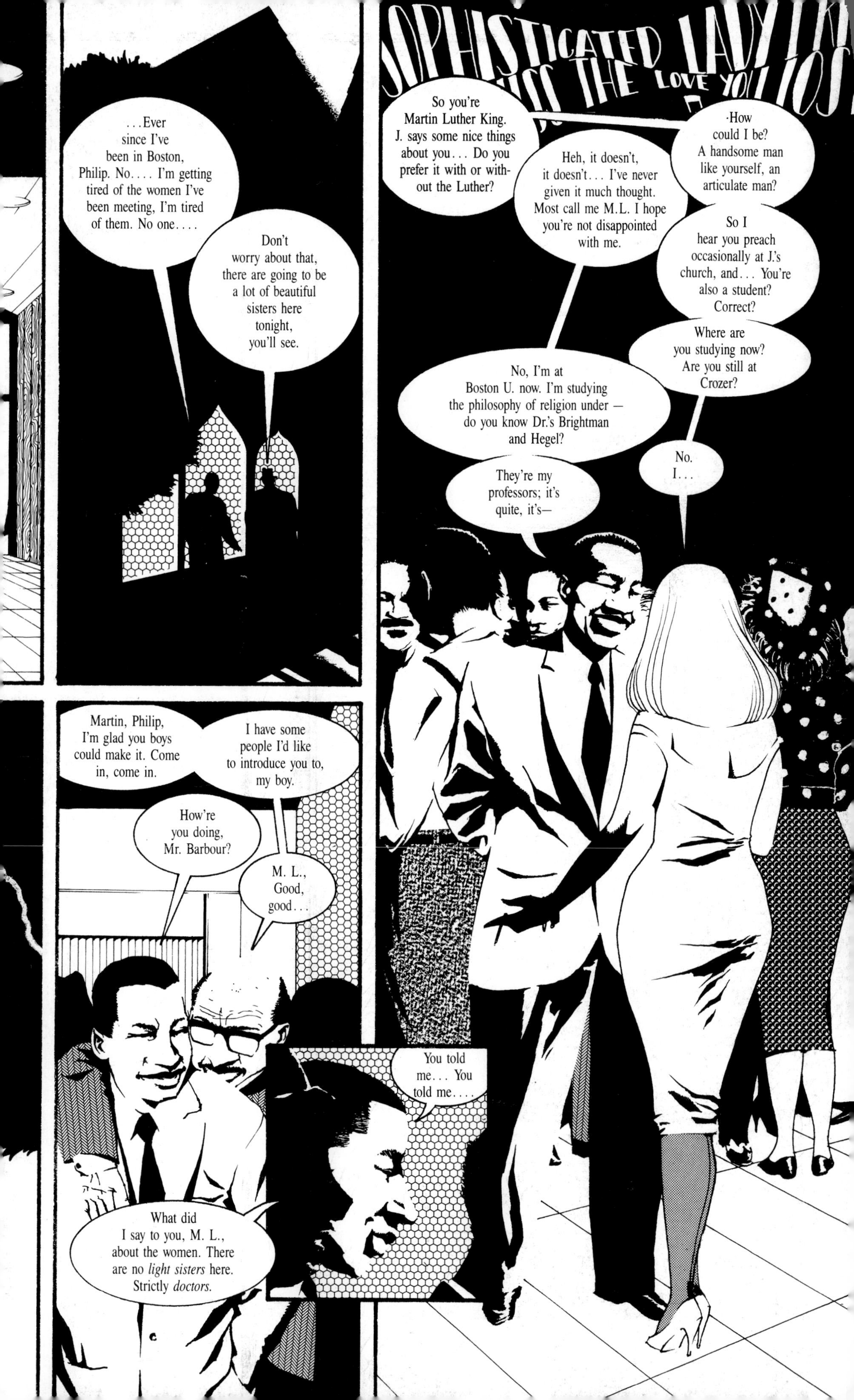
...Ever since I've been in Boston, Philip. No.... I'm getting tired of the women I've been meeting, I'm tired of them. No one....
Don't worry about that, there are going to be a lot of beautiful sisters here tonight, you'll see.
Martin, Philip, I'm glad you boys could make it. Come in, come in.
I have some people I'd like to introduce you to, my boy.
How're you doing, Mr. Barbour?
M. L., Good, good...
What did I say to you, M. L., about the women. There are no *light sisters* here. Strictly *doctors.*
You told me... You told me....
SOPHISTICATED LADY
THE LOVE YOU
So you're Martin Luther King. J. says some nice things about you... Do you prefer it with or without the Luther?
Heh, it doesn't, it doesn't... I've never given it much thought. Most call me M.L. I hope you're not disappointed with me.
·How could I be? A handsome man like yourself, an articulate man?
So I hear you preach occasionally at J.'s church, and... You're also a student? Correct?
Where are you studying now? Are you still at Crozer?
No, I'm at Boston U. now. I'm studying the philosophy of religion under — do you know Dr.'s Brightman and Hegel?
No. I...
They're my professors; it's quite, it's—

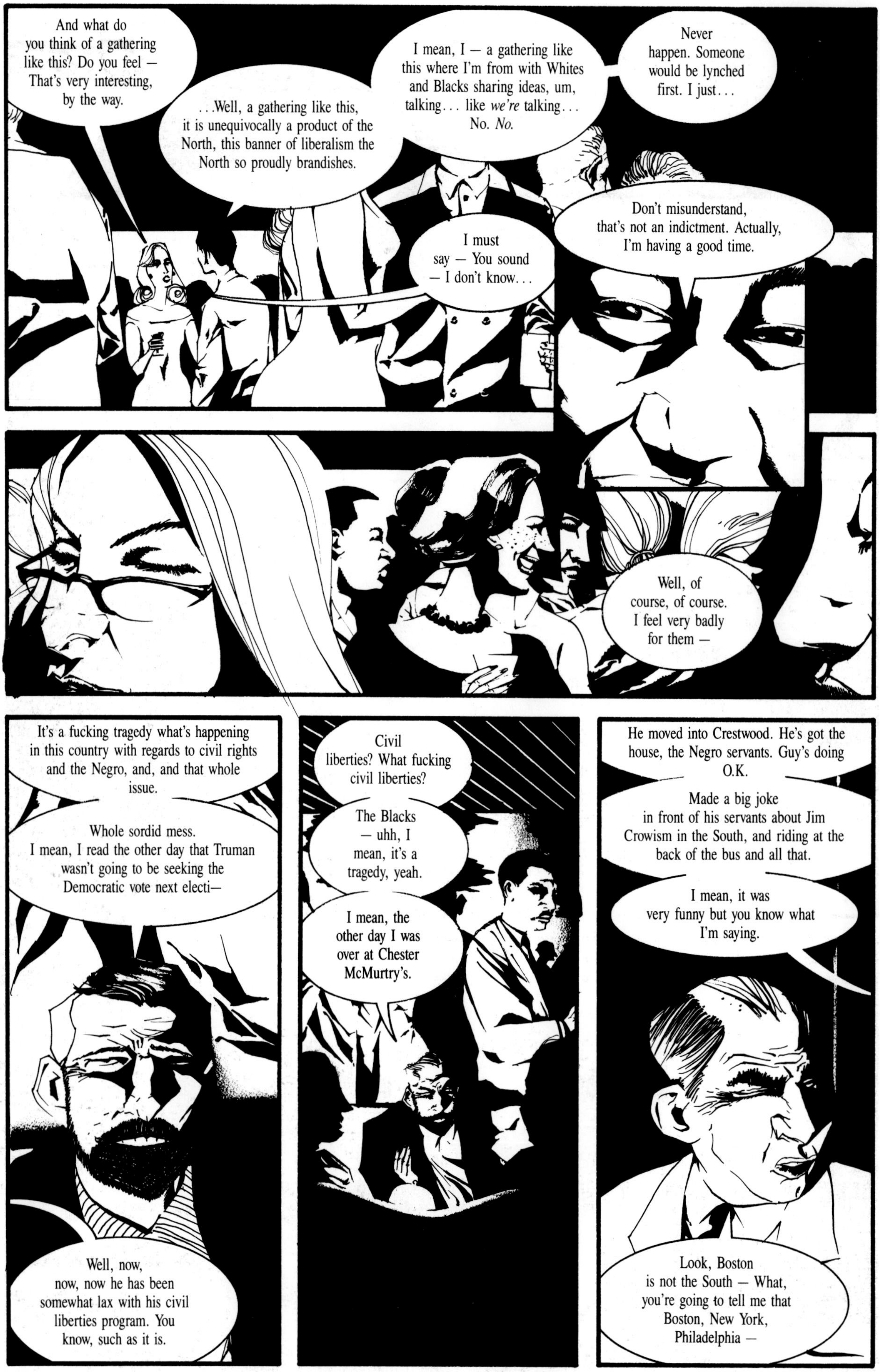
And what do you think of a gathering like this? Do you feel — That's very interesting, by the way.
. . .Well, a gathering like this, it is unequivocally a product of the North, this banner of liberalism the North so proudly brandishes.
I mean, I — a gathering like this where I'm from with Whites and Blacks sharing ideas, um, talking. . . like *we're* talking. . . No. *No.*
Never happen. Someone would be lynched first. I just. . .
I must say — You sound — I don't know. . .
Don't misunderstand, that's not an indictment. Actually, I'm having a good time.
Well, of course, of course. I feel very badly for them —
It's a fucking tragedy what's happening in this country with regards to civil rights and the Negro, and, and that whole issue.
Whole sordid mess. I mean, I read the other day that Truman wasn't going to be seeking the Democratic vote next electi—
Well, now, now, now he has been somewhat lax with his civil liberties program. You know, such as it is.
Civil liberties? What fucking civil liberties?
The Blacks — uhh, I mean, it's a tragedy, yeah.
I mean, the other day I was over at Chester McMurtry's.
He moved into Crestwood. He's got the house, the Negro servants. Guy's doing O.K.
Made a big joke in front of his servants about Jim Crowism in the South, and riding at the back of the bus and all that.
I mean, it was very funny but you know what I'm saying.
Look, Boston is not the South — What, you're going to tell me that Boston, New York, Philadelphia —

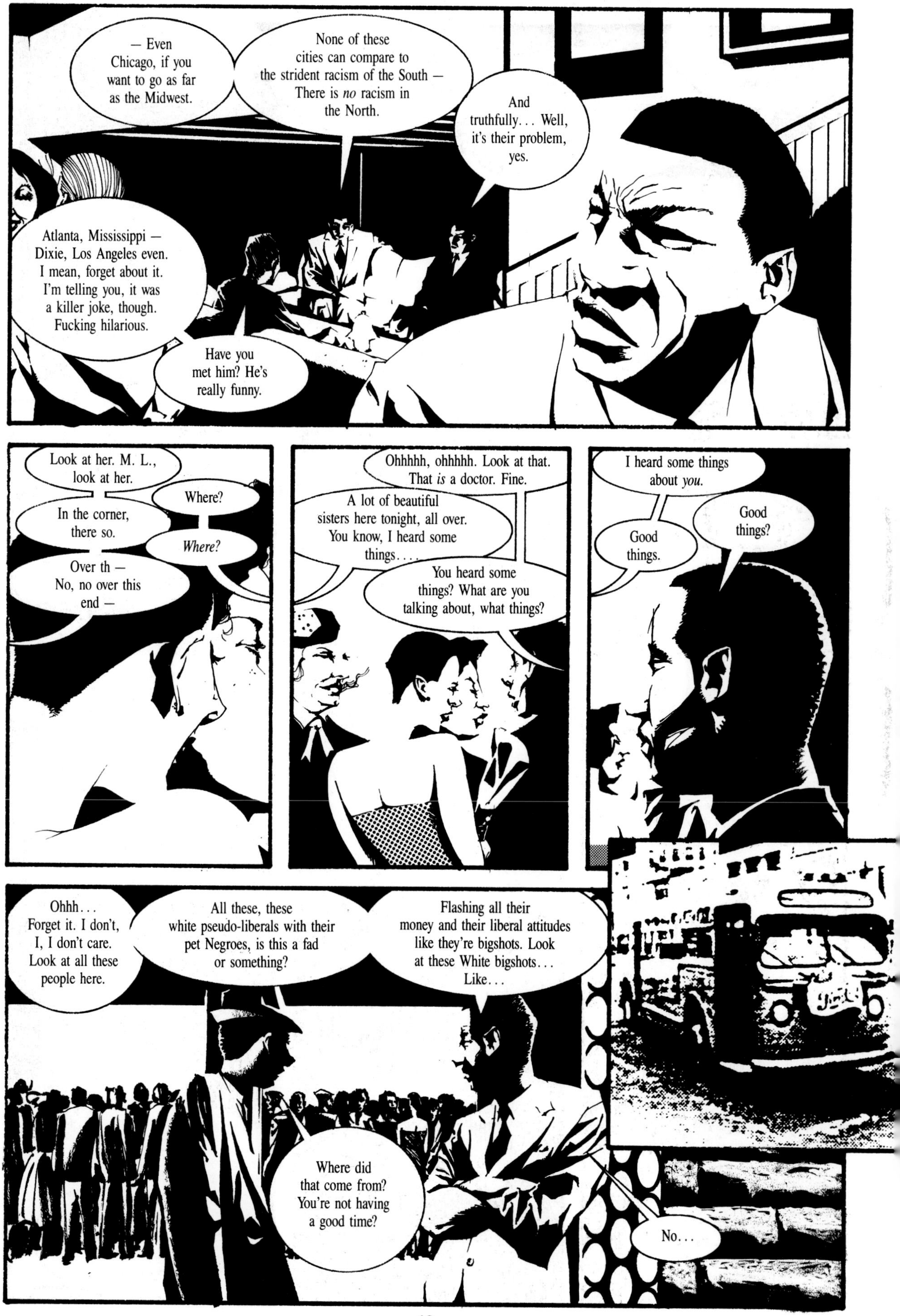
— Even Chicago, if you want to go as far as the Midwest.
None of these cities can compare to the strident racism of the South — There is *no* racism in the North.
And truthfully... Well, it's their problem, yes.
Atlanta, Mississippi — Dixie, Los Angeles even. I mean, forget about it. I'm telling you, it was a killer joke, though. Fucking hilarious.
Have you met him? He's really funny.
Look at her. M. L., look at her.
Where?
In the corner, there so.
Where?
Over th — No, no over this end —
Ohhhhh, ohhhhh. Look at that. That *is* a doctor. Fine.
A lot of beautiful sisters here tonight, all over. You know, I heard some things....
You heard some things? What are you talking about, what things?
I heard some things about *you.*
Good things.
Good things?
Ohhh... Forget it. I don't, I, I don't care. Look at all these people here.
All these, these white pseudo-liberals with their pet Negroes, is this a fad or something?
Flashing all their money and their liberal attitudes like they're bigshots. Look at these White bigshots... Like...
Where did that come from? You're not having a good time?
No...

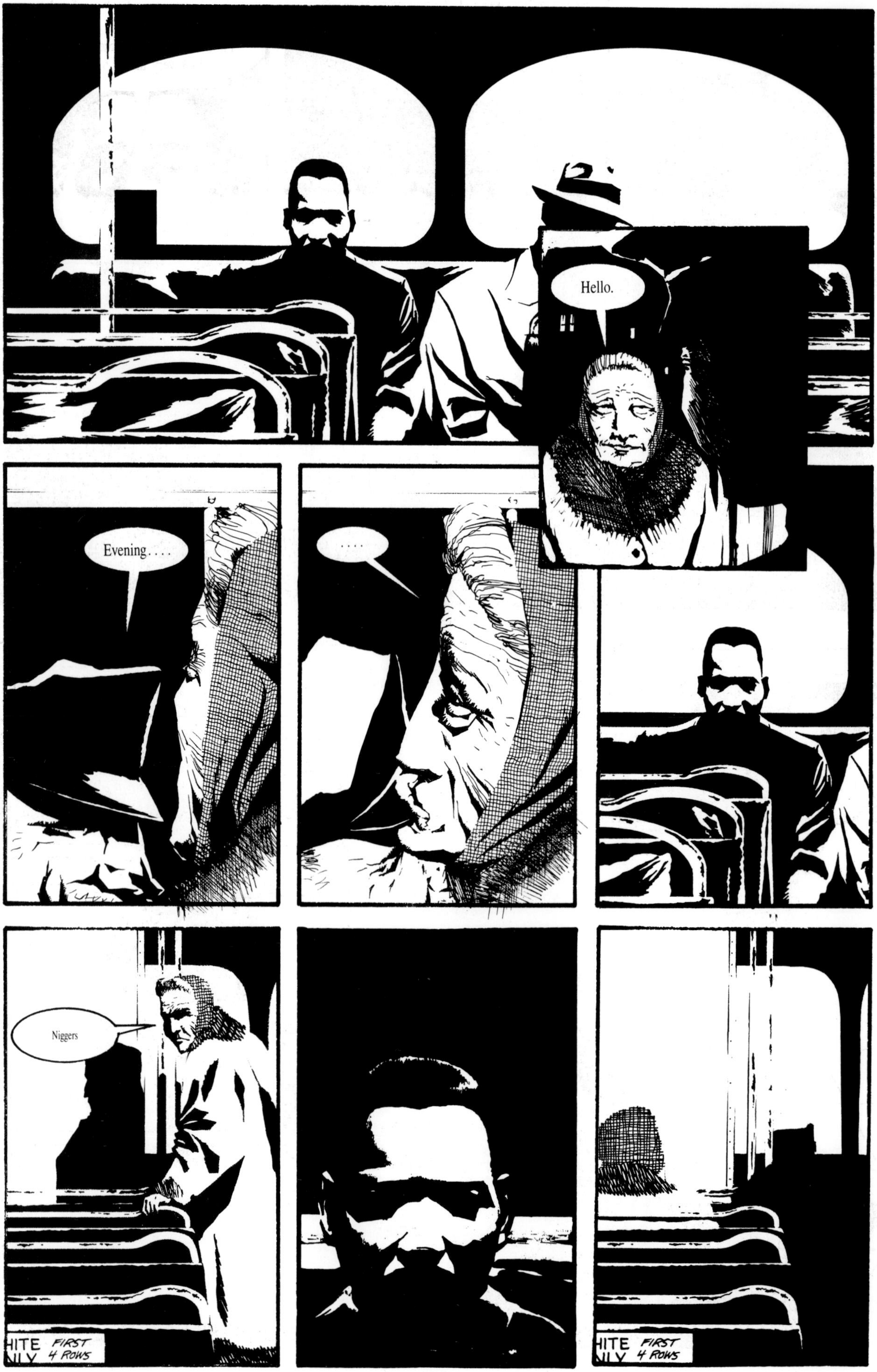
Hello.
Evening....
....
Niggers
HITE FIRST
NLY 4 ROWS
HITE FIRST
NLY 4 ROWS

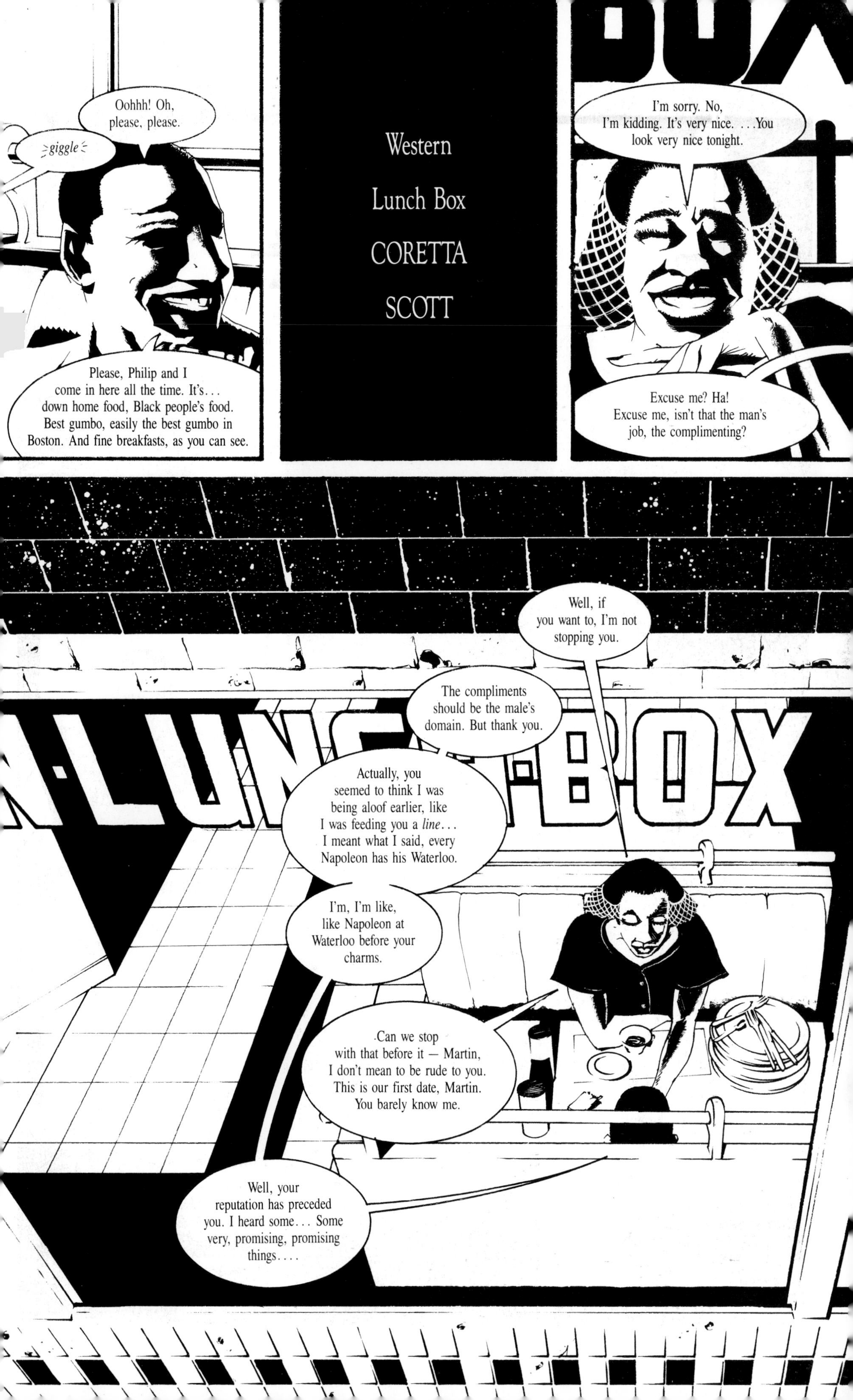
giggle
Oohhh! Oh, please, please.
Please, Philip and I come in here all the time. It's... down home food, Black people's food. Best gumbo, easily the best gumbo in Boston. And fine breakfasts, as you can see.
Western
Lunch Box
CORETTA
SCOTT
I'm sorry. No, I'm kidding. It's very nice. . . .You look very nice tonight.
Excuse me? Ha! Excuse me, isn't that the man's job, the complimenting?
Well, if you want to, I'm not stopping you.
The compliments should be the male's domain. But thank you.
Actually, you seemed to think I was being aloof earlier, like I was feeding you a *line*... I meant what I said, every Napoleon has his Waterloo.
I'm, I'm like, like Napoleon at Waterloo before your charms.
Can we stop with that before it — Martin, I don't mean to be rude to you. This is our first date, Martin. You barely know me.
Well, your reputation has preceded you. I heard some... Some very, promising, promising things....

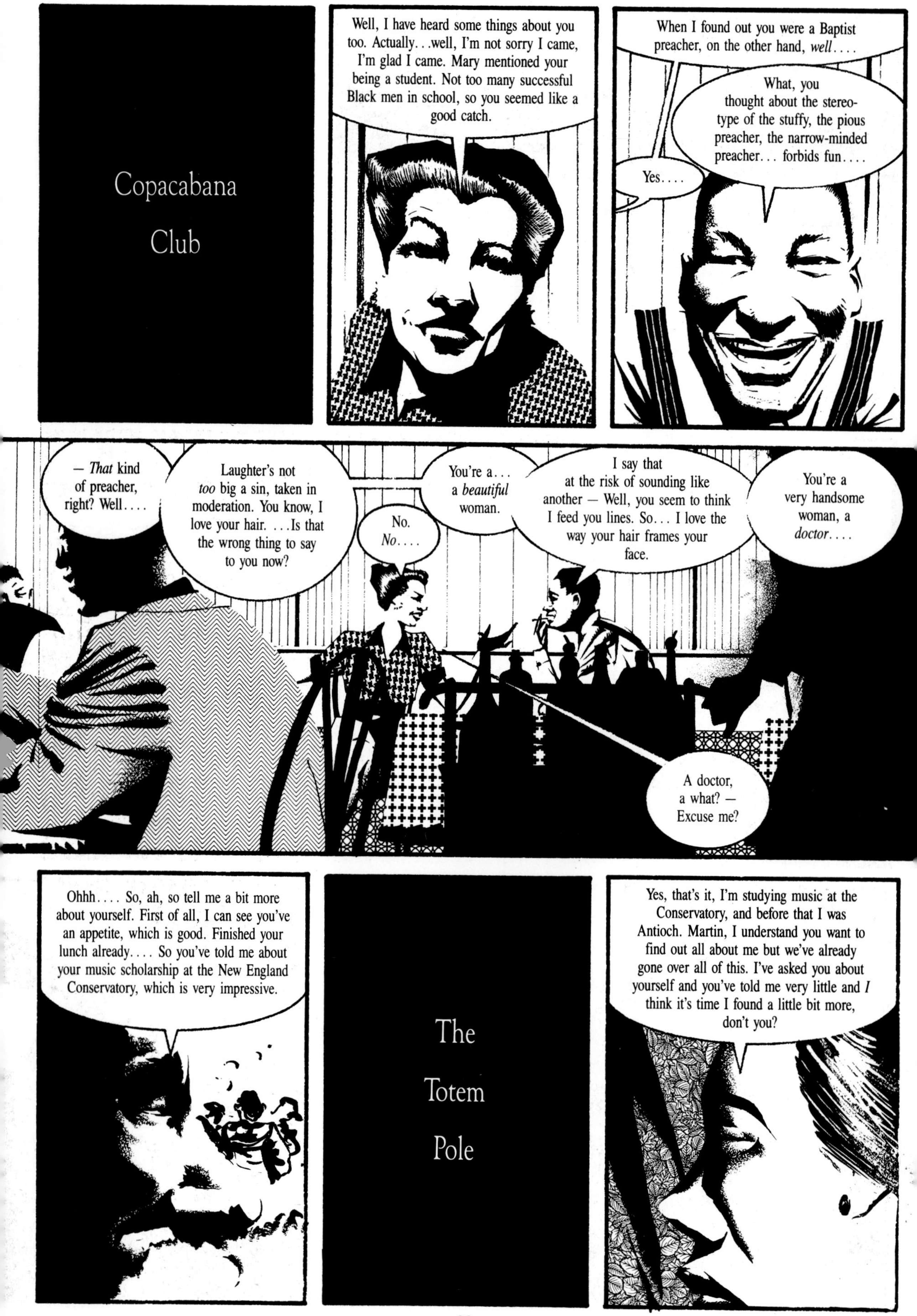
Copacabana Club
Well, I have heard some things about you too. Actually...well, I'm not sorry I came, I'm glad I came. Mary mentioned your being a student. Not too many successful Black men in school, so you seemed like a good catch.
When I found out you were a Baptist preacher, on the other hand, *well*....
What, you thought about the stereotype of the stuffy, the pious preacher, the narrow-minded preacher... forbids fun....
Yes....
— *That* kind of preacher, right? Well....
Laughter's not *too* big a sin, taken in moderation. You know, I love your hair. ...Is that the wrong thing to say to you now?
No. *No*....
You're a... a *beautiful* woman.
I say that at the risk of sounding like another — Well, you seem to think I feed you lines. So... I love the way your hair frames your face.
You're a very handsome woman, a *doctor*....
A doctor, a what? — Excuse me?
Ohhh.... So, ah, so tell me a bit more about yourself. First of all, I can see you've an appetite, which is good. Finished your lunch already.... So you've told me about your music scholarship at the New England Conservatory, which is very impressive.
The Totem Pole
Yes, that's it, I'm studying music at the Conservatory, and before that I was Antioch. Martin, I understand you want to find out all about me but we've already gone over all of this. I've asked you about yourself and you've told me very little and *I* think it's time I found a little bit more, don't you?

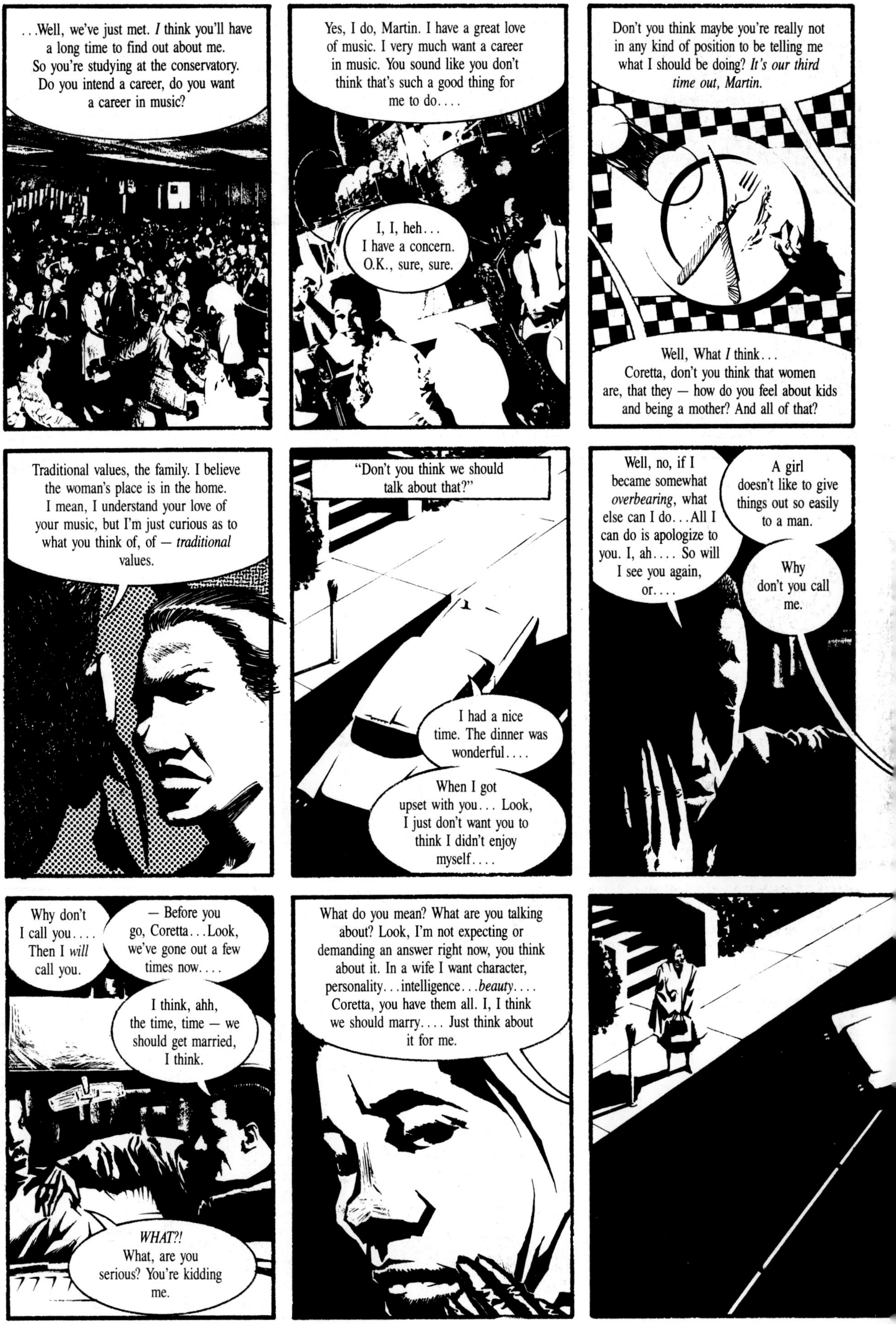
. . .Well, we've just met. *I* think you'll have a long time to find out about me. So you're studying at the conservatory. Do you intend a career, do you want a career in music?
Yes, I do, Martin. I have a great love of music. I very much want a career in music. You sound like you don't think that's such a good thing for me to do. . . .
I, I, heh. . . I have a concern. O.K., sure, sure.
Don't you think maybe you're really not in any kind of position to be telling me what I should be doing? *It's our third time out, Martin.*
Well, What *I* think. . . Coretta, don't you think that women are, that they — how do you feel about kids and being a mother? And all of that?
Traditional values, the family. I believe the woman's place is in the home. I mean, I understand your love of your music, but I'm just curious as to what you think of, of — *traditional* values.
"Don't you think we should talk about that?"
I had a nice time. The dinner was wonderful. . . .
When I got upset with you. . . Look, I just don't want you to think I didn't enjoy myself. . . .
Well, no, if I became somewhat *overbearing*, what else can I do. . . All I can do is apologize to you. I, ah. . . . So will I see you again, or. . . .
A girl doesn't like to give things out so easily to a man.
Why don't you call me.
Why don't I call you. . . . Then I *will* call you.
— Before you go, Coretta. . . Look, we've gone out a few times now. . . .
I think, ahh, the time, time — we should get married, I think.
WHAT?! What, are you serious? You're kidding me.
What do you mean? What are you talking about? Look, I'm not expecting or demanding an answer right now, you think about it. In a wife I want character, personality. . . intelligence. . . *beauty*. . . . Coretta, you have them all. I, I think we should marry. . . . Just think about it for me.

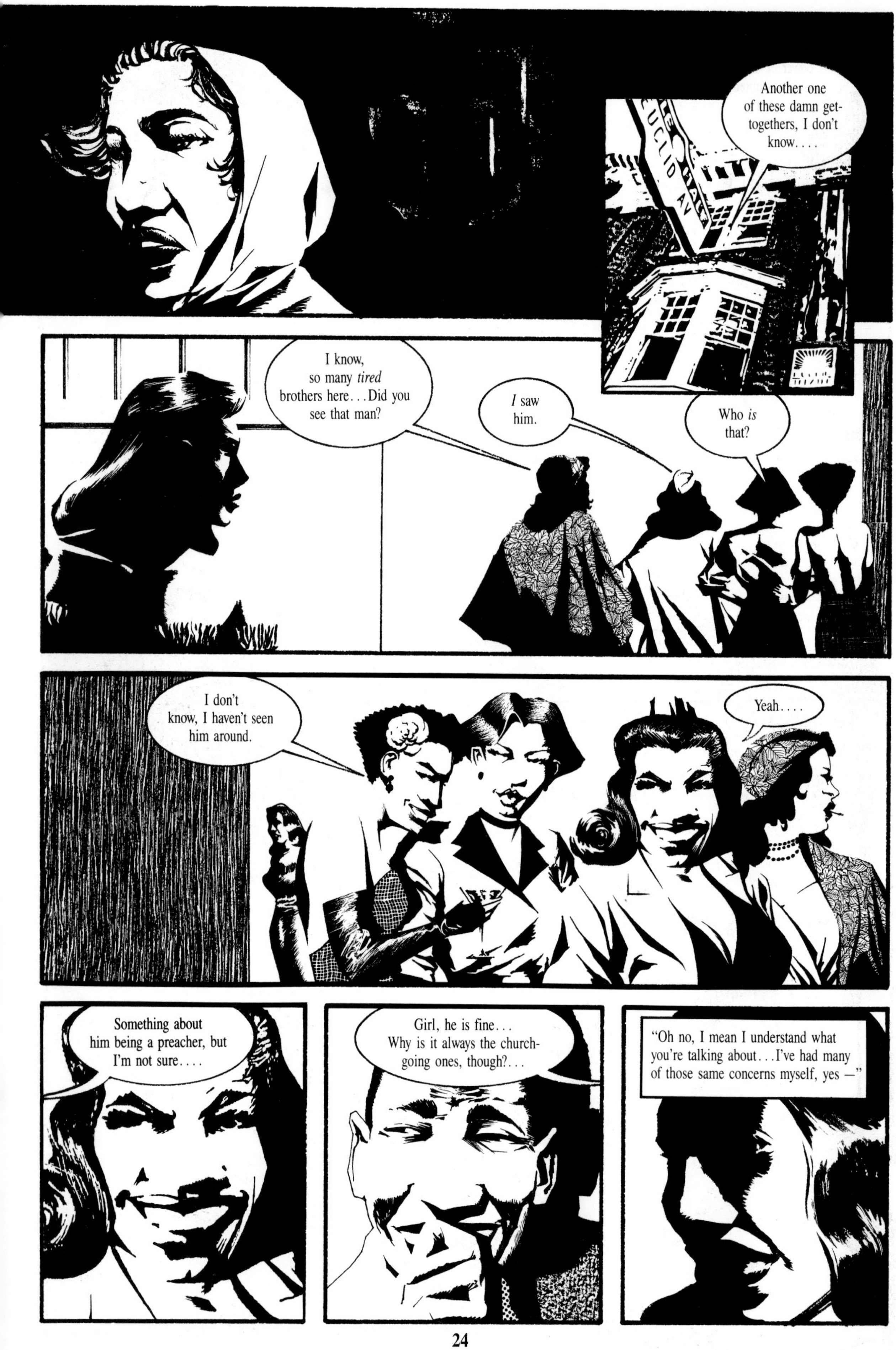
Another one of these damn get-togethers, I don't know. . . .
I know, so many *tired* brothers here. . .Did you see that man?
I saw him.
Who *is* that?
I don't know, I haven't seen him around.
Yeah. . . .
Something about him being a preacher, but I'm not sure. . . .
Girl, he is fine. . . Why is it always the church-going ones, though?. . .
"Oh no, I mean I understand what you're talking about. . .I've had many of those same concerns myself, yes —"

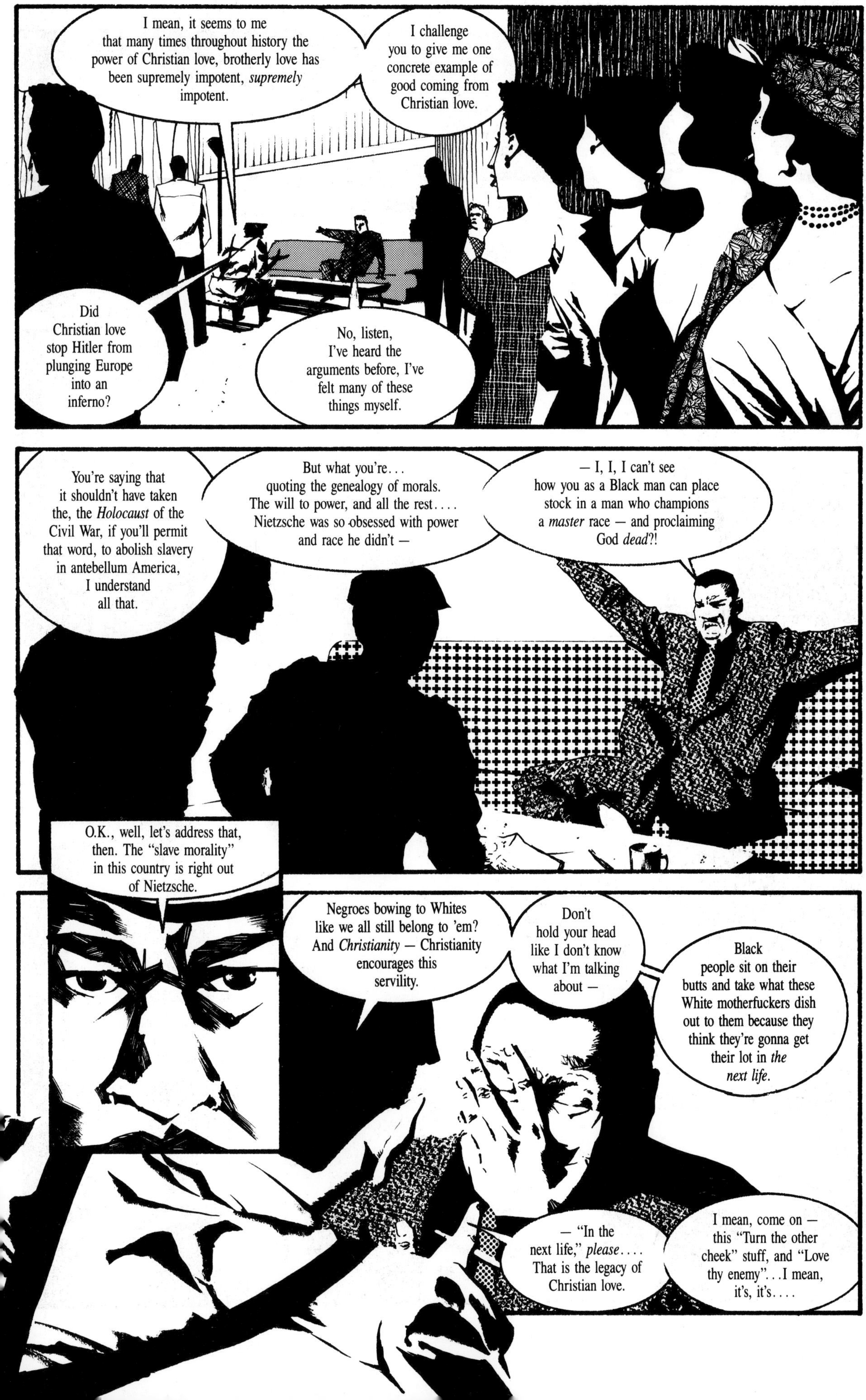

I mean, it seems to me that many times throughout history the power of Christian love, brotherly love has been supremely impotent, *supremely* impotent.
I challenge you to give me one concrete example of good coming from Christian love.
Did Christian love stop Hitler from plunging Europe into an inferno?
No, listen, I've heard the arguments before, I've felt many of these things myself.
You're saying that it shouldn't have taken the, the *Holocaust* of the Civil War, if you'll permit that word, to abolish slavery in antebellum America, I understand all that.
But what you're... quoting the genealogy of morals. The will to power, and all the rest.... Nietzsche was so obsessed with power and race he didn't —
— I, I, I can't see how you as a Black man can place stock in a man who champions a *master* race — and proclaiming God *dead*?!
O.K., well, let's address that, then. The "slave morality" in this country is right out of Nietzsche.
Negroes bowing to Whites like we all still belong to 'em? And *Christianity* — Christianity encourages this servility.
Don't hold your head like I don't know what I'm talking about —
Black people sit on their butts and take what these White motherfuckers dish out to them because they think they're gonna get their lot in *the next life*.
— "In the next life," *please*.... That is the legacy of Christian love.
I mean, come on — this "Turn the other cheek" stuff, and "Love thy enemy"...I mean, it's, it's....

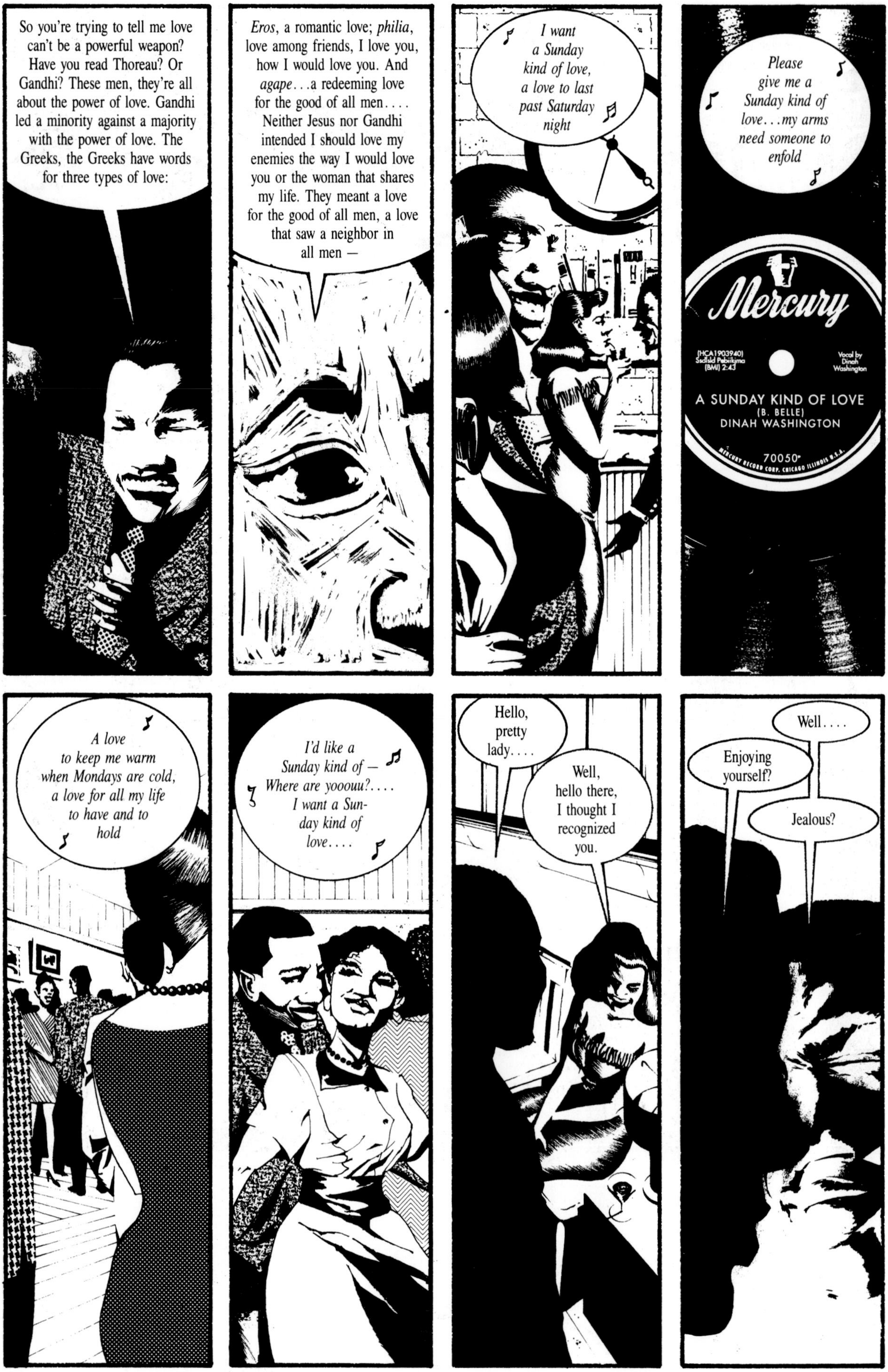

So you're trying to tell me love can't be a powerful weapon? Have you read Thoreau? Or Gandhi? These men, they're all about the power of love. Gandhi led a minority against a majority with the power of love. The Greeks, the Greeks have words for three types of love:
Eros, a romantic love; *philia*, love among friends, I love you, how I would love you. And *agape*...a redeeming love for the good of all men.... Neither Jesus nor Gandhi intended I should love my enemies the way I would love you or the woman that shares my life. They meant a love for the good of all men, a love that saw a neighbor in all men —
I want a Sunday kind of love, a love to last past Saturday night
Please give me a Sunday kind of love...my arms need someone to enfold
Mercury
Vocal by Dinah Washington
A SUNDAY KIND OF LOVE
(B. BELLE)
DINAH WASHINGTON
70050
MERCURY RECORD CORP. CHICAGO ILLINOIS U.S.A.
A love to keep me warm when Mondays are cold, a love for all my life to have and to hold
I'd like a Sunday kind of — Where are yooouu?.... I want a Sunday kind of love....
Hello, pretty lady....
Well, hello there, I thought I recognized you.
Enjoying yourself?
Well....
Jealous?

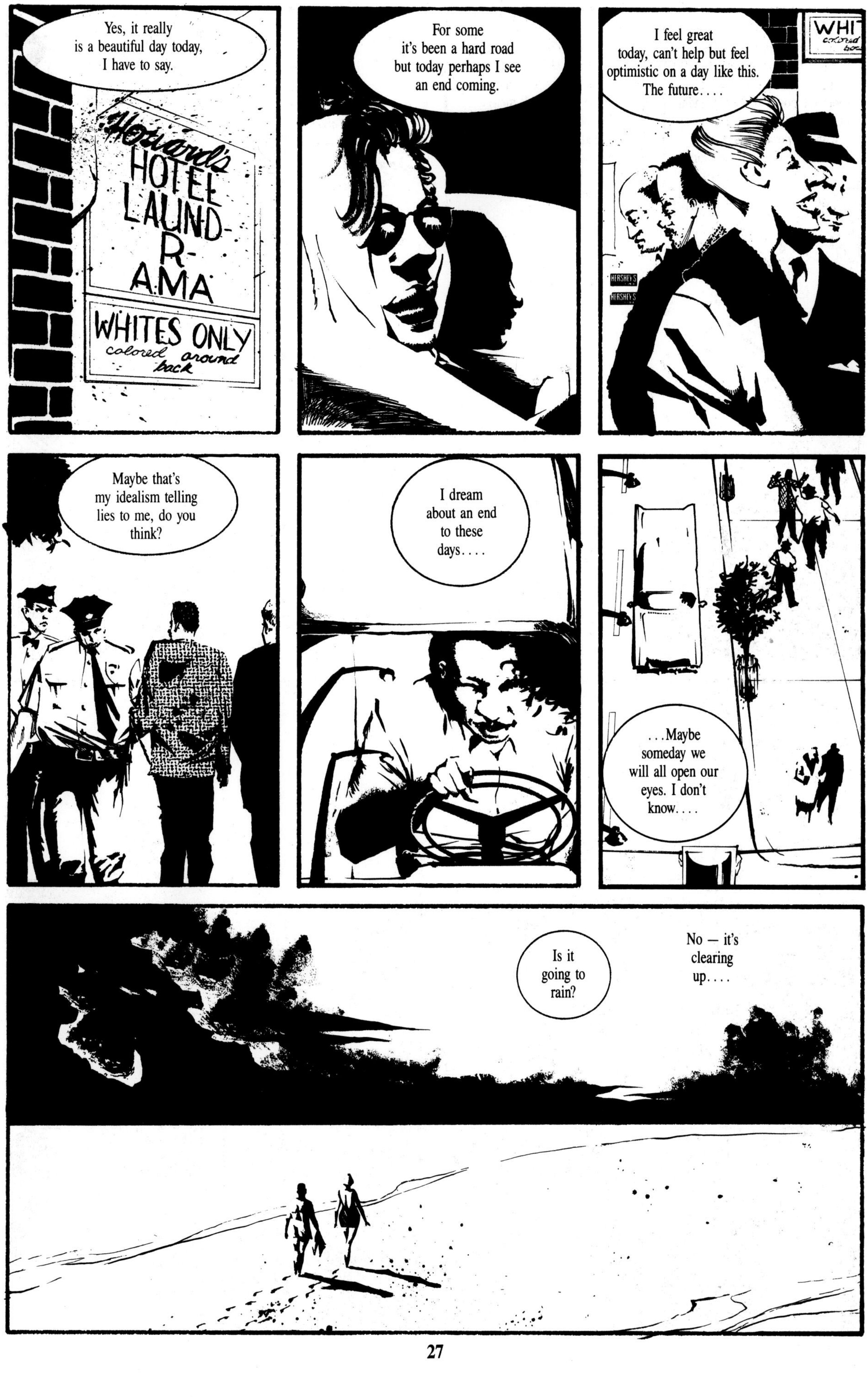
Yes, it really is a beautiful day today, I have to say.
Howard's HOTEL LAUND-R-AMA
WHITES ONLY colored around back
For some it's been a hard road but today perhaps I see an end coming.
I feel great today, can't help but feel optimistic on a day like this. The future. . . .
HERSHEY'S
HERSHEY'S
Maybe that's my idealism telling lies to me, do you think?
I dream about an end to these days. . . .
. . .Maybe someday we will all open our eyes. I don't know. . . .
Is it going to rain?
No — it's clearing up. . . .

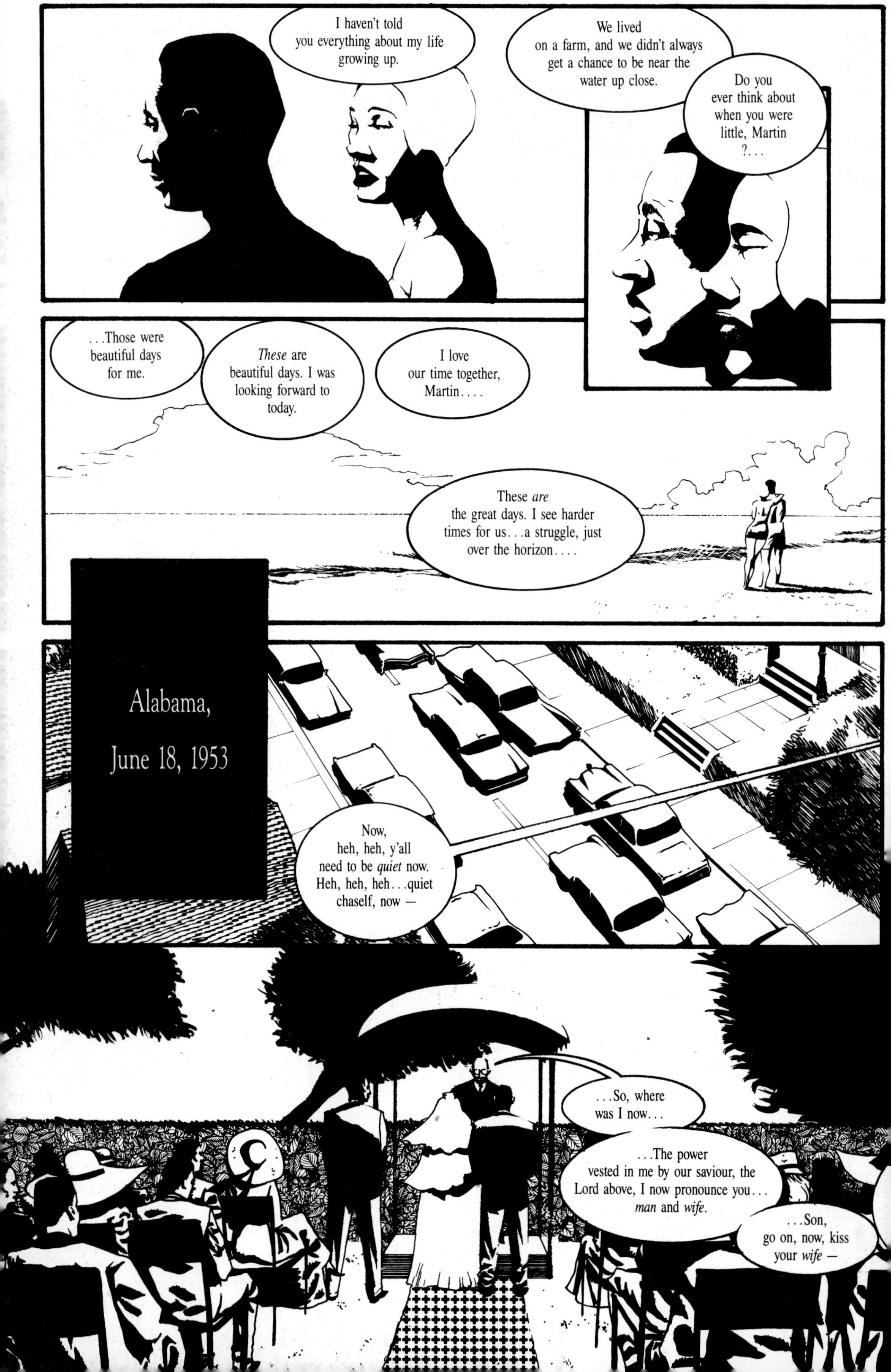
I haven't told you everything about my life growing up.
We lived on a farm, and we didn't always get a chance to be near the water up close.
Do you ever think about when you were little, Martin ?. . .
. . .Those were beautiful days for me.
These are beautiful days. I was looking forward to today.
I love our time together, Martin. . . .
These *are* the great days. I see harder times for us. . .a struggle, just over the horizon. . . .
Alabama, June 18, 1953
Now, heh, heh, y'all need to be *quiet* now. Heh, heh, heh. . .quiet chaself, now —
. . .So, where was I now. . .
. . .The power vested in me by our saviour, the Lord above, I now pronounce you. . . *man* and *wife*.
. . .Son, go on, now, kiss your *wife* —

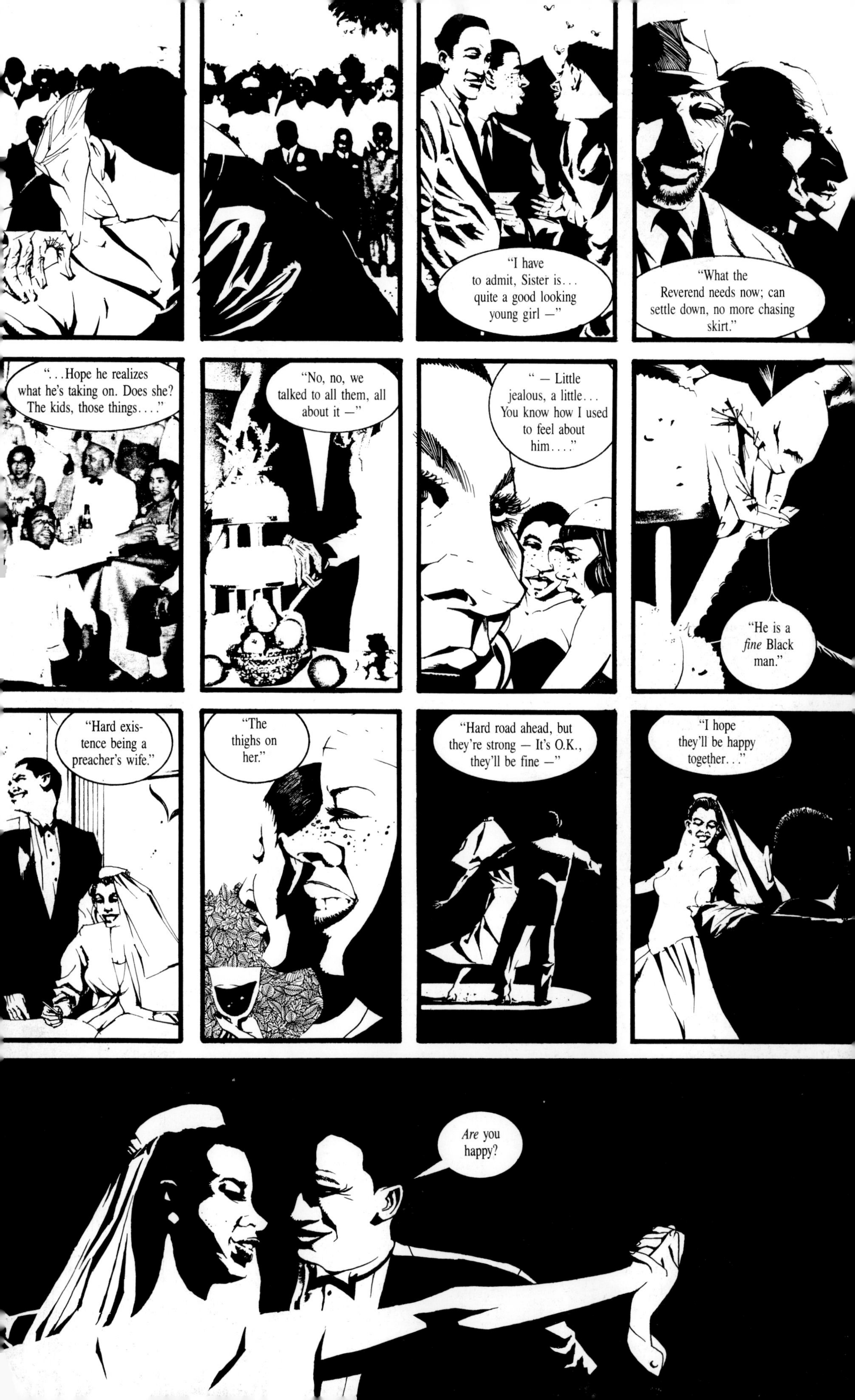
"I have
to admit, Sister is...
quite a good looking
young girl —"
"What the
Reverend needs now; can
settle down, no more chasing
skirt."
"...Hope he realizes
what he's taking on. Does she?
The kids, those things...."
"No, no, we
talked to all them, all
about it —"
" — Little
jealous, a little...
You know how I used
to feel about
him...."
"He is a
fine Black
man."
"Hard exis-
tence being a
preacher's wife."
"The
thighs on
her."
"Hard road ahead, but
they're strong — It's O.K.,
they'll be fine —"
"I hope
they'll be happy
together..."
Are you
happy?

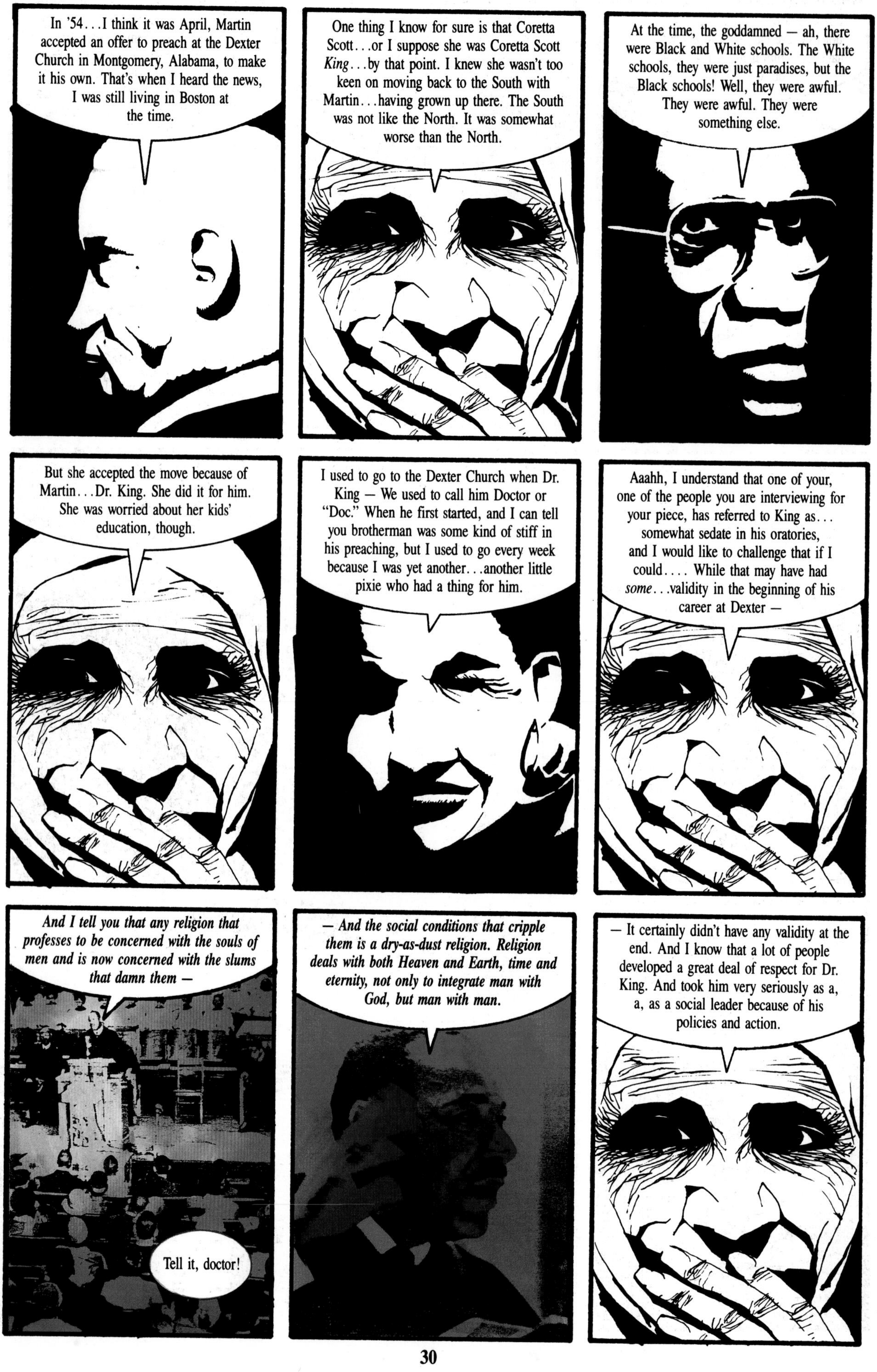
In '54...I think it was April, Martin accepted an offer to preach at the Dexter Church in Montgomery, Alabama, to make it his own. That's when I heard the news, I was still living in Boston at the time.
One thing I know for sure is that Coretta Scott...or I suppose she was Coretta Scott *King*...by that point. I knew she wasn't too keen on moving back to the South with Martin...having grown up there. The South was not like the North. It was somewhat worse than the North.
At the time, the goddamned — ah, there were Black and White schools. The White schools, they were just paradises, but the Black schools! Well, they were awful. They were awful. They were something else.
But she accepted the move because of Martin...Dr. King. She did it for him. She was worried about her kids' education, though.
I used to go to the Dexter Church when Dr. King — We used to call him Doctor or "Doc." When he first started, and I can tell you brotherman was some kind of stiff in his preaching, but I used to go every week because I was yet another...another little pixie who had a thing for him.
Aaahh, I understand that one of your, one of the people you are interviewing for your piece, has referred to King as... somewhat sedate in his oratories, and I would like to challenge that if I could.... While that may have had *some*...validity in the beginning of his career at Dexter —
And I tell you that any religion that professes to be concerned with the souls of men and is now concerned with the slums that damn them —
Tell it, doctor!
— And the social conditions that cripple them is a dry-as-dust religion. Religion deals with both Heaven and Earth, time and eternity, not only to integrate man with God, but man with man.
— It certainly didn't have any validity at the end. And I know that a lot of people developed a great deal of respect for Dr. King. And took him very seriously as a, a, as a social leader because of his policies and action.

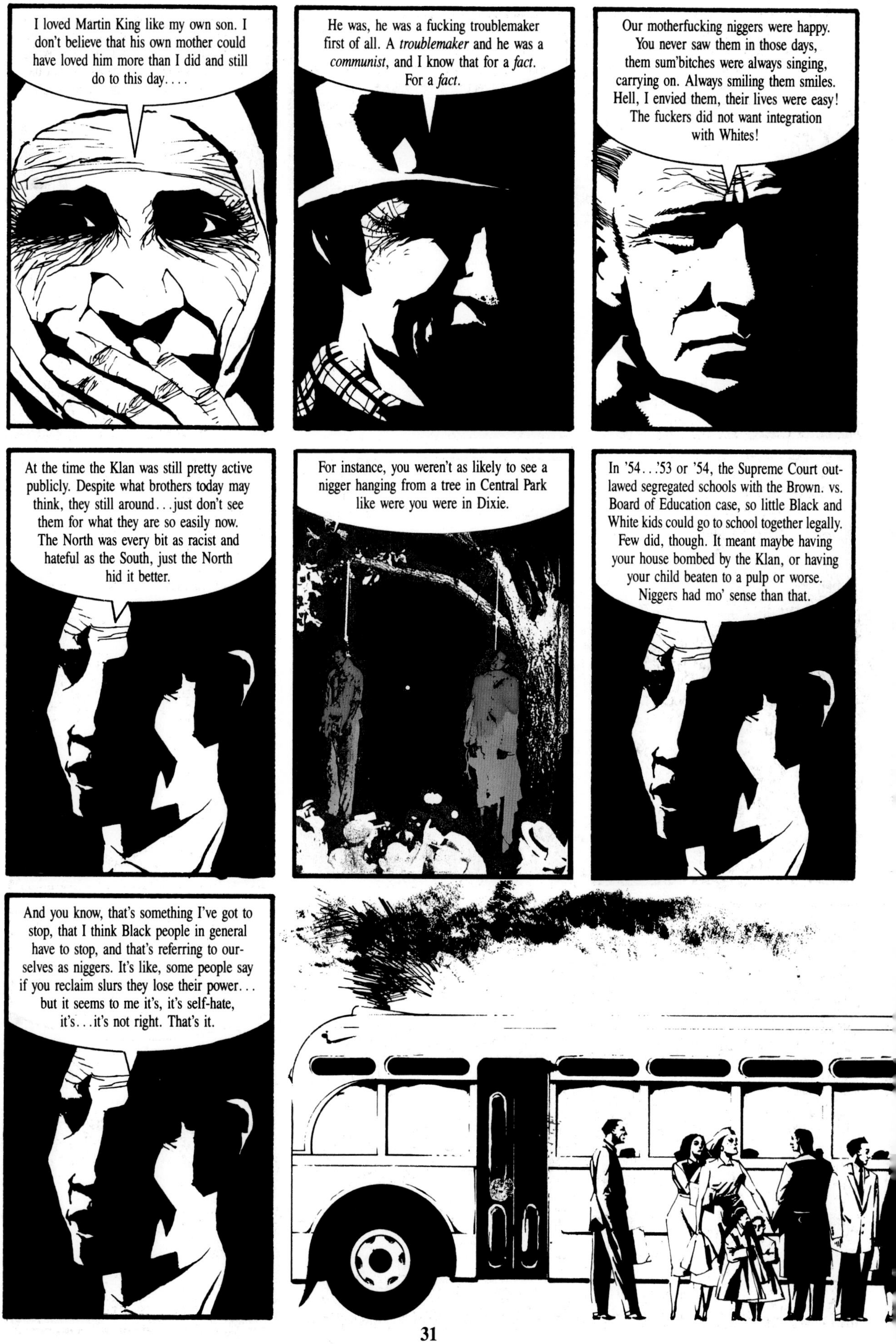
I loved Martin King like my own son. I don't believe that his own mother could have loved him more than I did and still do to this day....
He was, he was a fucking troublemaker first of all. A *troublemaker* and he was a *communist*, and I know that for a *fact*. For a *fact*.
Our motherfucking niggers were happy. You never saw them in those days, them sum'bitches were always singing, carrying on. Always smiling them smiles. Hell, I envied them, their lives were easy! The fuckers did not want integration with Whites!
At the time the Klan was still pretty active publicly. Despite what brothers today may think, they still around...just don't see them for what they are so easily now. The North was every bit as racist and hateful as the South, just the North hid it better.
For instance, you weren't as likely to see a nigger hanging from a tree in Central Park like were you were in Dixie.
In '54...'53 or '54, the Supreme Court outlawed segregated schools with the Brown. vs. Board of Education case, so little Black and White kids could go to school together legally. Few did, though. It meant maybe having your house bombed by the Klan, or having your child beaten to a pulp or worse. Niggers had mo' sense than that.
And you know, that's something I've got to stop, that I think Black people in general have to stop, and that's referring to ourselves as niggers. It's like, some people say if you reclaim slurs they lose their power... but it seems to me it's, it's self-hate, it's...it's not right. That's it.

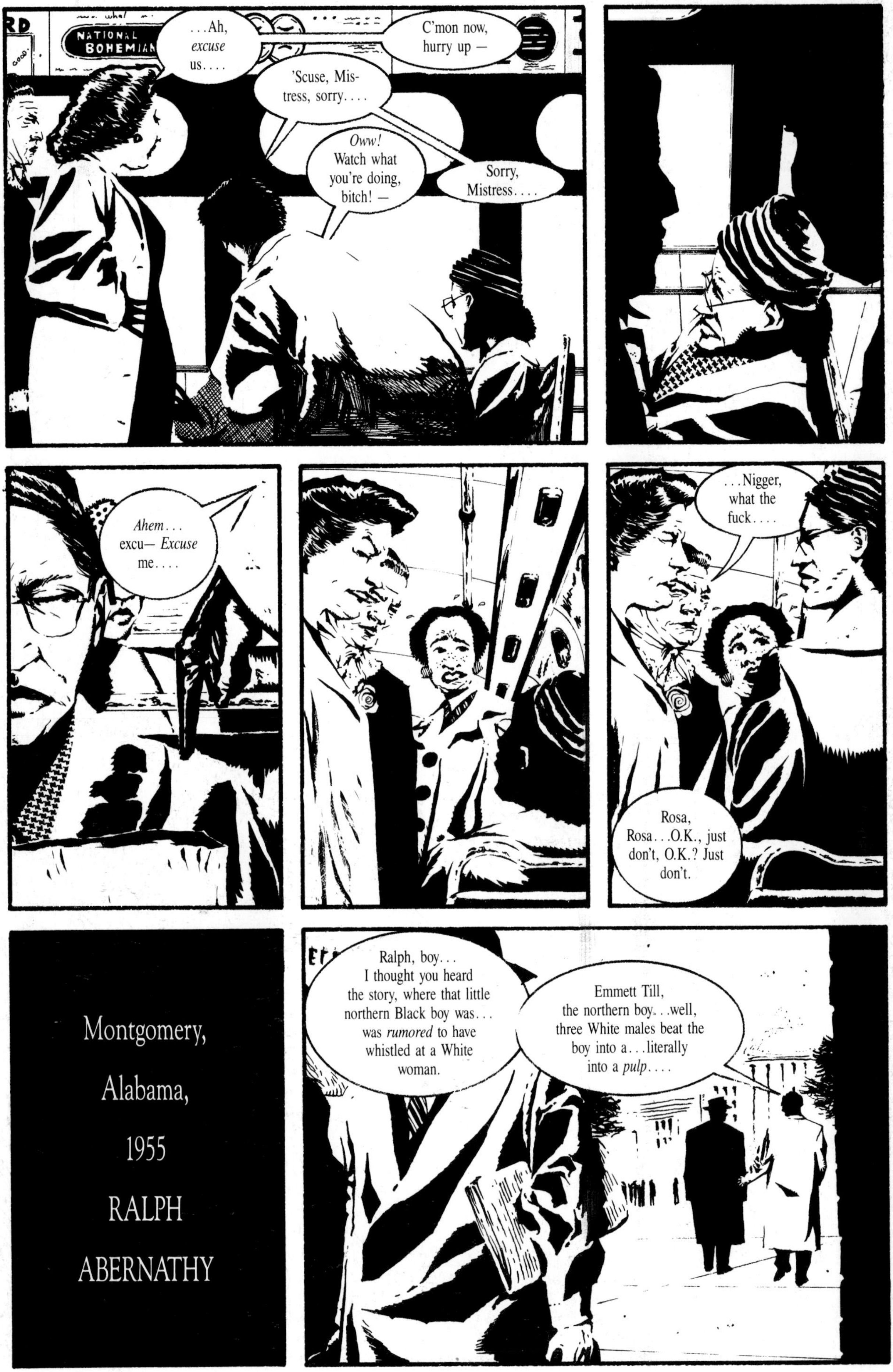

...Ah, *excuse* us....
C'mon now, hurry up —
'Scuse, Mistress, sorry....
Oww! Watch what you're doing, bitch! —
Sorry, Mistress....
Ahem... excu— *Excuse* me....
...Nigger, what the fuck....
Rosa, Rosa...O.K., just don't, O.K.? Just don't.
Montgomery, Alabama, 1955
RALPH ABERNATHY
Ralph, boy... I thought you heard the story, where that little northern Black boy was... was *rumored* to have whistled at a White woman.
Emmett Till, the northern boy...well, three White males beat the boy into a...literally into a *pulp*....

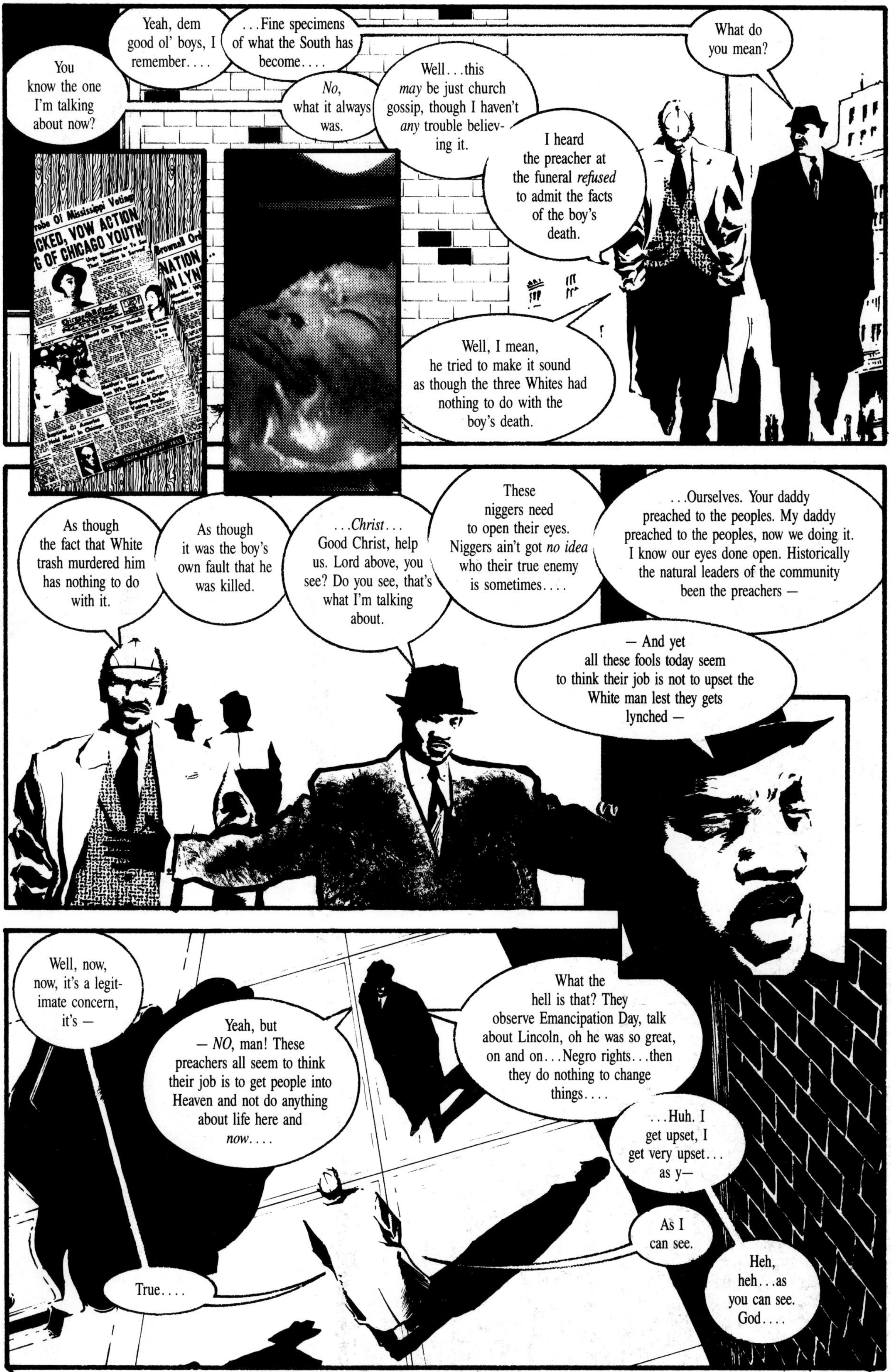

You know the one I'm talking about now?
Yeah, dem good ol' boys, I remember. . . .
. . .Fine specimens of what the South has become. . . .
No, what it always was.
Well. . .this *may* be just church gossip, though I haven't *any* trouble believ-ing it.
I heard the preacher at the funeral *refused* to admit the facts of the boy's death.
What do you mean?
Well, I mean, he tried to make it sound as though the three Whites had nothing to do with the boy's death.
As though the fact that White trash murdered him has nothing to do with it.
As though it was the boy's own fault that he was killed.
. . .*Christ*. . . Good Christ, help us. Lord above, you see? Do you see, that's what I'm talking about.
These niggers need to open their eyes. Niggers ain't got *no idea* who their true enemy is sometimes. . . .
. . .Ourselves. Your daddy preached to the peoples. My daddy preached to the peoples, now we doing it. I know our eyes done open. Historically the natural leaders of the community been the preachers —
— And yet all these fools today seem to think their job is not to upset the White man lest they gets lynched —
Well, now, now, it's a legit-imate concern, it's —
Yeah, but — *NO*, man! These preachers all seem to think their job is to get people into Heaven and not do anything about life here and *now*. . . .
What the hell is that? They observe Emancipation Day, talk about Lincoln, oh he was so great, on and on. . .Negro rights. . .then they do nothing to change things. . . .
. . .Huh. I get upset, I get very upset. . . as y—
As I can see.
True. . . .
Heh, heh. . .as you can see. God. . . .

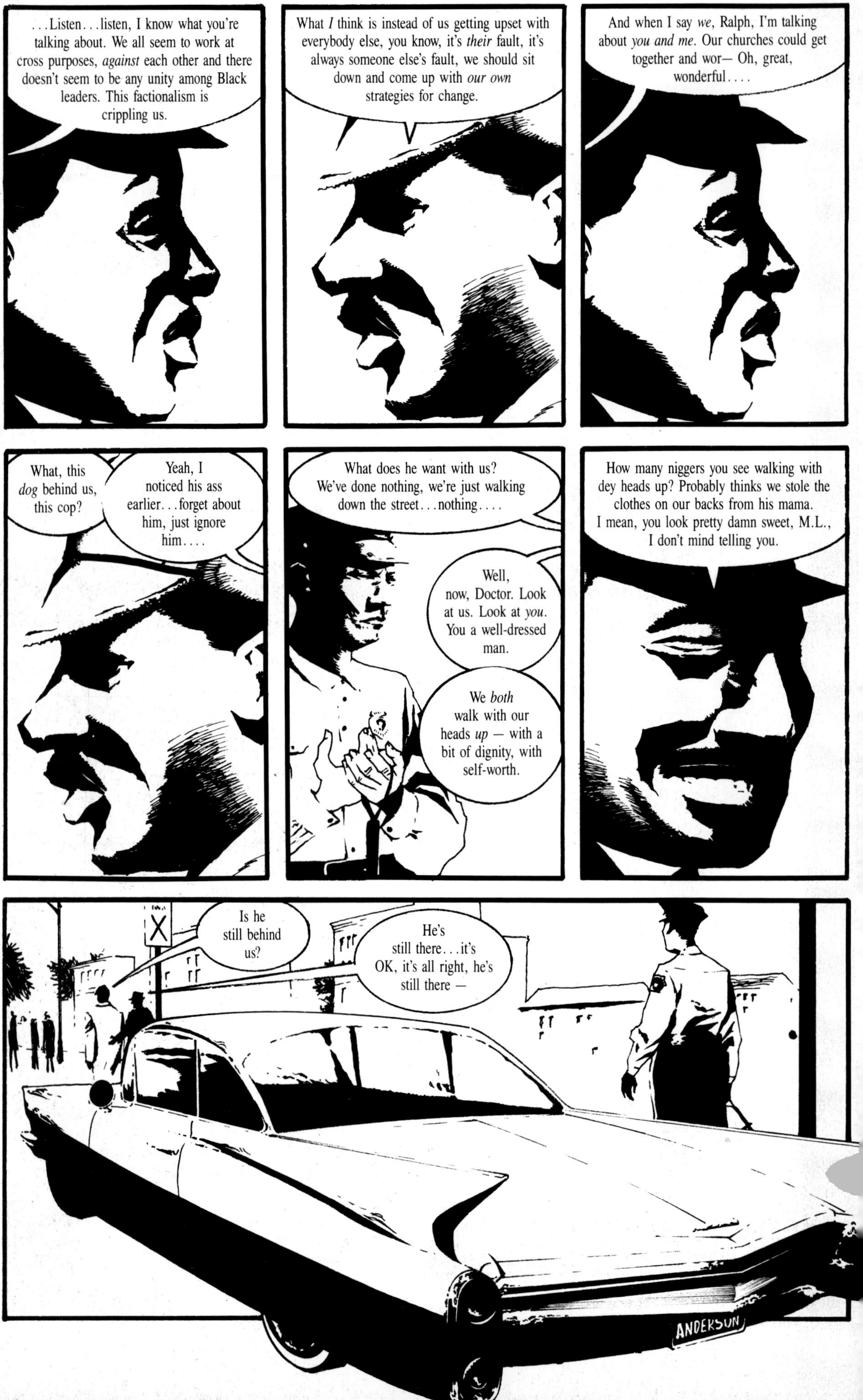
. . .Listen. . .listen, I know what you're talking about. We all seem to work at cross purposes, *against* each other and there doesn't seem to be any unity among Black leaders. This factionalism is crippling us.
What *I* think is instead of us getting upset with everybody else, you know, it's *their* fault, it's always someone else's fault, we should sit down and come up with *our own* strategies for change.
And when I say *we*, Ralph, I'm talking about *you and me*. Our churches could get together and wor— Oh, great, wonderful. . . .
What, this *dog* behind us, this cop?
Yeah, I noticed his ass earlier. . .forget about him, just ignore him. . . .
What does he want with us? We've done nothing, we're just walking down the street. . .nothing. . . .
Well, now, Doctor. Look at us. Look at *you*. You a well-dressed man.
We *both* walk with our heads *up* — with a bit of dignity, with self-worth.
How many niggers you see walking with dey heads up? Probably thinks we stole the clothes on our backs from his mama. I mean, you look pretty damn sweet, M.L., I don't mind telling you.
Is he still behind us?
He's still there. . .it's OK, it's all right, he's still there —
ANDERSON

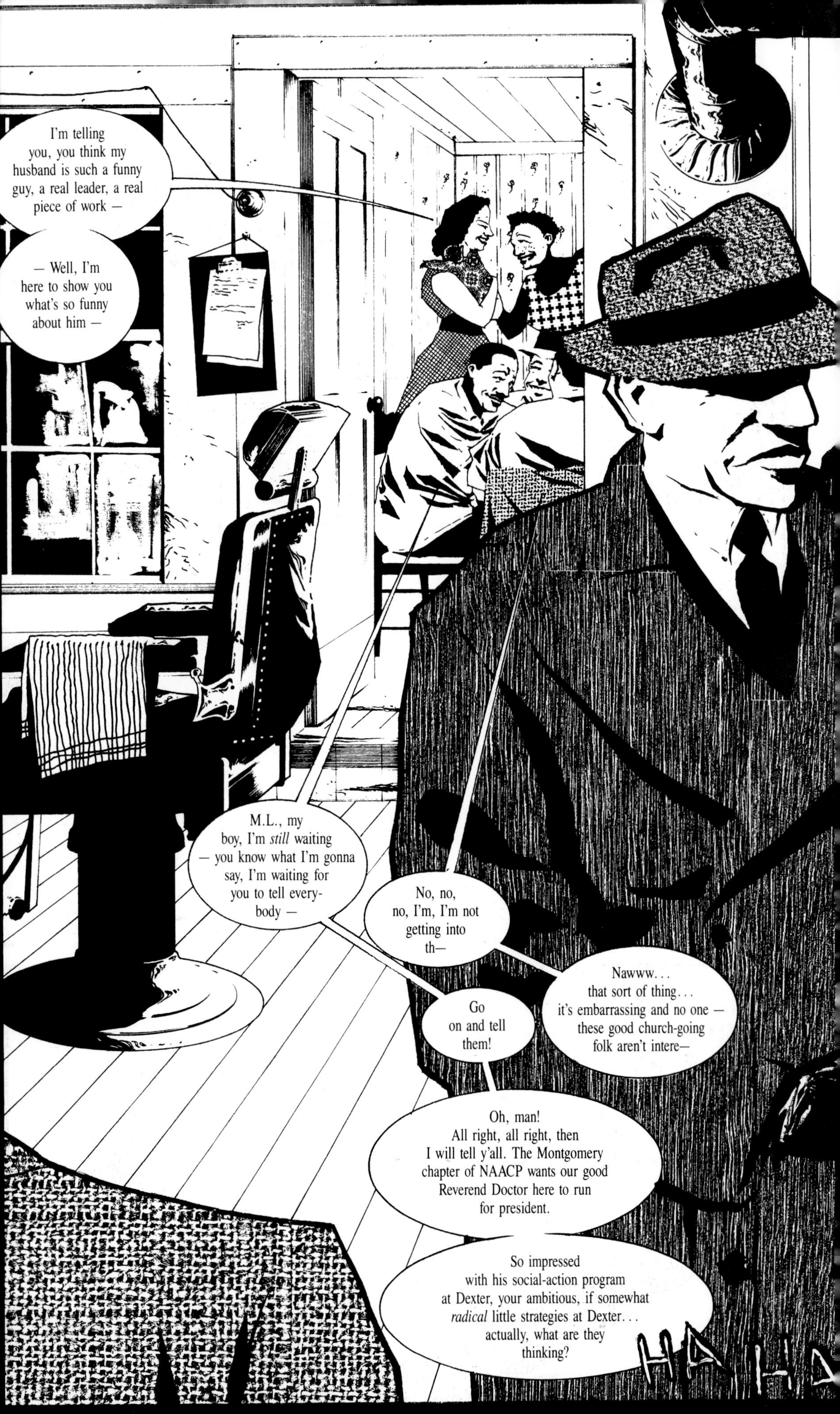
I'm telling you, you think my husband is such a funny guy, a real leader, a real piece of work —
— Well, I'm here to show you what's so funny about him —
M.L., my boy, I'm *still* waiting — you know what I'm gonna say, I'm waiting for you to tell every-body —
No, no, no, I'm, I'm not getting into th—
Go on and tell them!
Nawww... that sort of thing... it's embarrassing and no one — these good church-going folk aren't intere—
Oh, man! All right, all right, then I will tell y'all. The Montgomery chapter of NAACP wants our good Reverend Doctor here to run for president.
So impressed with his social-action program at Dexter, your ambitious, if somewhat *radical* little strategies at Dexter... actually, what are they thinking?
HA HA

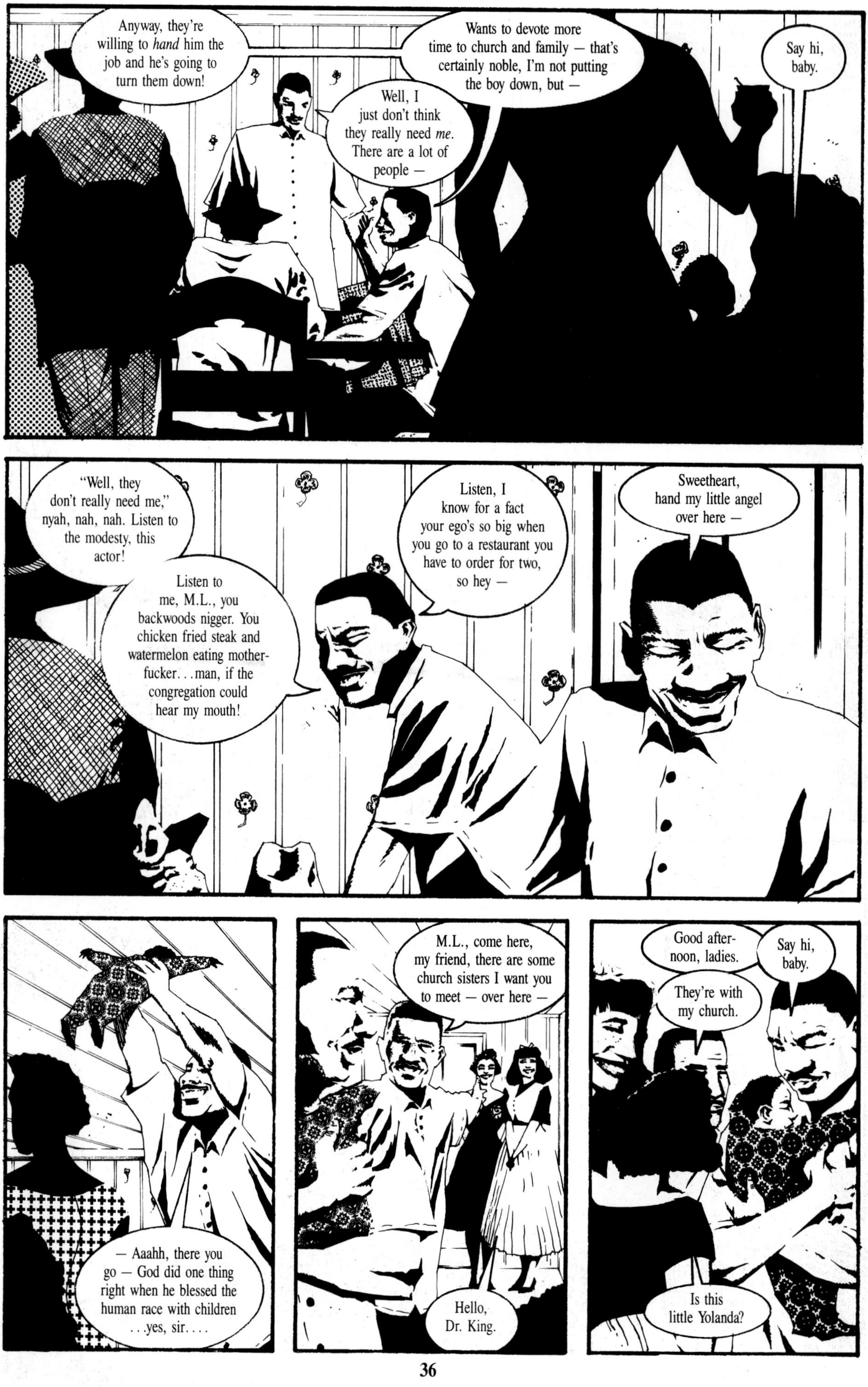
Anyway, they're willing to *hand* him the job and he's going to turn them down!
Wants to devote more time to church and family — that's certainly noble, I'm not putting the boy down, but —
Well, I just don't think they really need *me*. There are a lot of people —
Say hi, baby.
"Well, they don't really need me," nyah, nah, nah. Listen to the modesty, this actor!
Listen to me, M.L., you backwoods nigger. You chicken fried steak and watermelon eating mother-fucker. . .man, if the congregation could hear my mouth!
Listen, I know for a fact your ego's so big when you go to a restaurant you have to order for two, so hey —
Sweetheart, hand my little angel over here —
— Aaahh, there you go — God did one thing right when he blessed the human race with children . . .yes, sir. . . .
M.L., come here, my friend, there are some church sisters I want you to meet — over here —
Hello, Dr. King.
Good after-noon, ladies.
Say hi, baby.
They're with my church.
Is this little Yolanda?

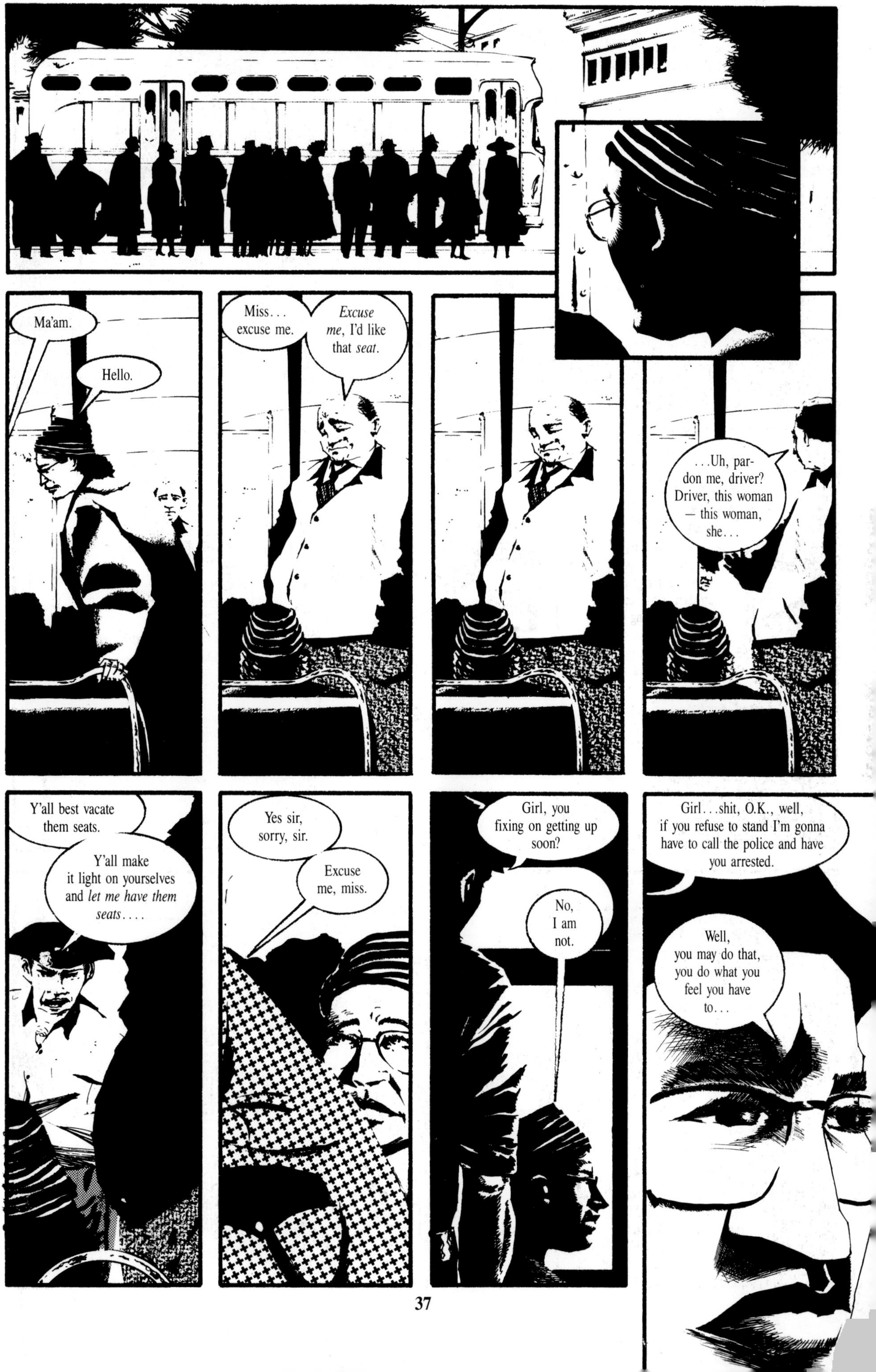
Ma'am.
Hello.
Miss... excuse me.
Excuse me, I'd like that *seat*.
...Uh, pardon me, driver? Driver, this woman — this woman, she...
Y'all best vacate them seats.
Y'all make it light on yourselves and *let me have them seats*....
Yes sir, sorry, sir.
Excuse me, miss.
Girl, you fixing on getting up soon?
No, I am not.
Girl...shit, O.K., well, if you refuse to stand I'm gonna have to call the police and have you arrested.
Well, you may do that, you do what you feel you have to...

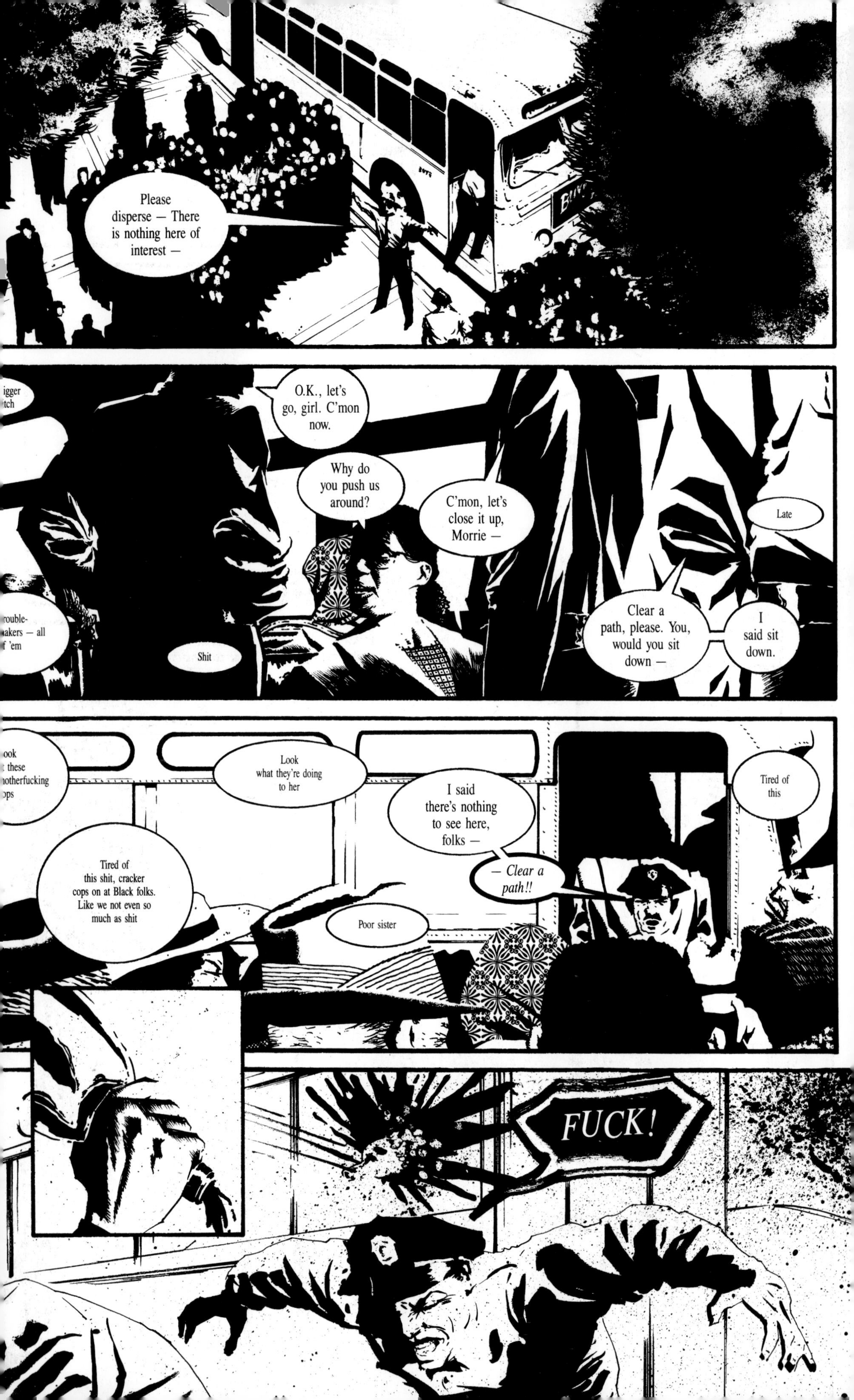
Please disperse — There is nothing here of interest —
igger
tch
O.K., let's go, girl. C'mon now.
Why do you push us around?
C'mon, let's close it up, Morrie —
Late
rouble-
akers — all
f 'em
Shit
Clear a path, please. You, would you sit down —
I said sit down.
ook
these
otherfucking
ops
Look what they're doing to her
I said there's nothing to see here, folks —
Tired of this
Tired of this shit, cracker cops on at Black folks. Like we not even so much as shit
— Clear a path!!
Poor sister
FUCK!

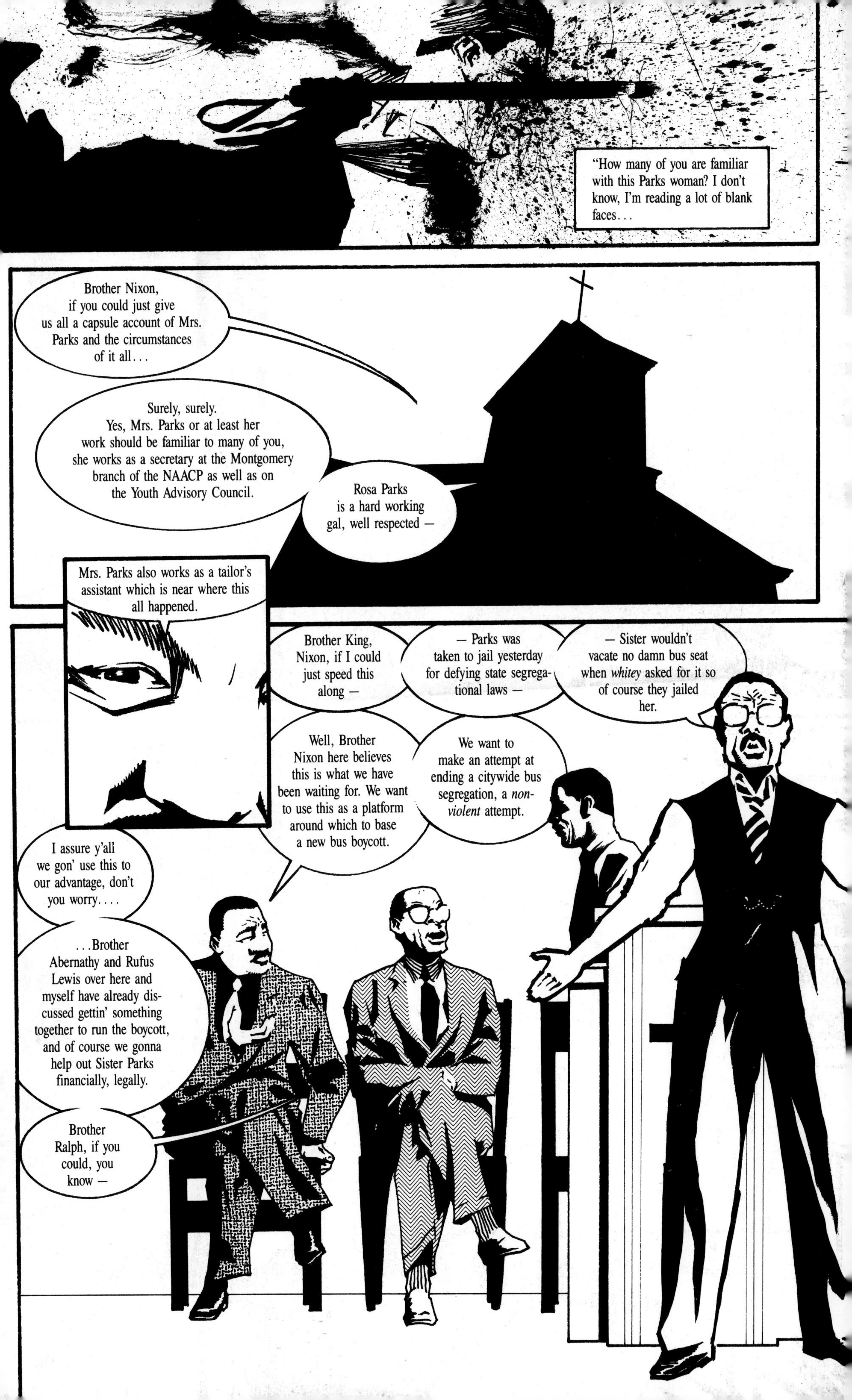
"How many of you are familiar with this Parks woman? I don't know, I'm reading a lot of blank faces. . .
Brother Nixon, if you could just give us all a capsule account of Mrs. Parks and the circumstances of it all. . .
Surely, surely. Yes, Mrs. Parks or at least her work should be familiar to many of you, she works as a secretary at the Montgomery branch of the NAACP as well as on the Youth Advisory Council.
Rosa Parks is a hard working gal, well respected —
Mrs. Parks also works as a tailor's assistant which is near where this all happened.
Brother King, Nixon, if I could just speed this along —
— Parks was taken to jail yesterday for defying state segregational laws —
— Sister wouldn't vacate no damn bus seat when *whitey* asked for it so of course they jailed her.
Well, Brother Nixon here believes this is what we have been waiting for. We want to use this as a platform around which to base a new bus boycott.
We want to make an attempt at ending a citywide bus segregation, a *non-violent* attempt.
I assure y'all we gon' use this to our advantage, don't you worry. . . .
. . .Brother Abernathy and Rufus Lewis over here and myself have already discussed gettin' something together to run the boycott, and of course we gonna help out Sister Parks financially, legally.
Brother Ralph, if you could, you know —

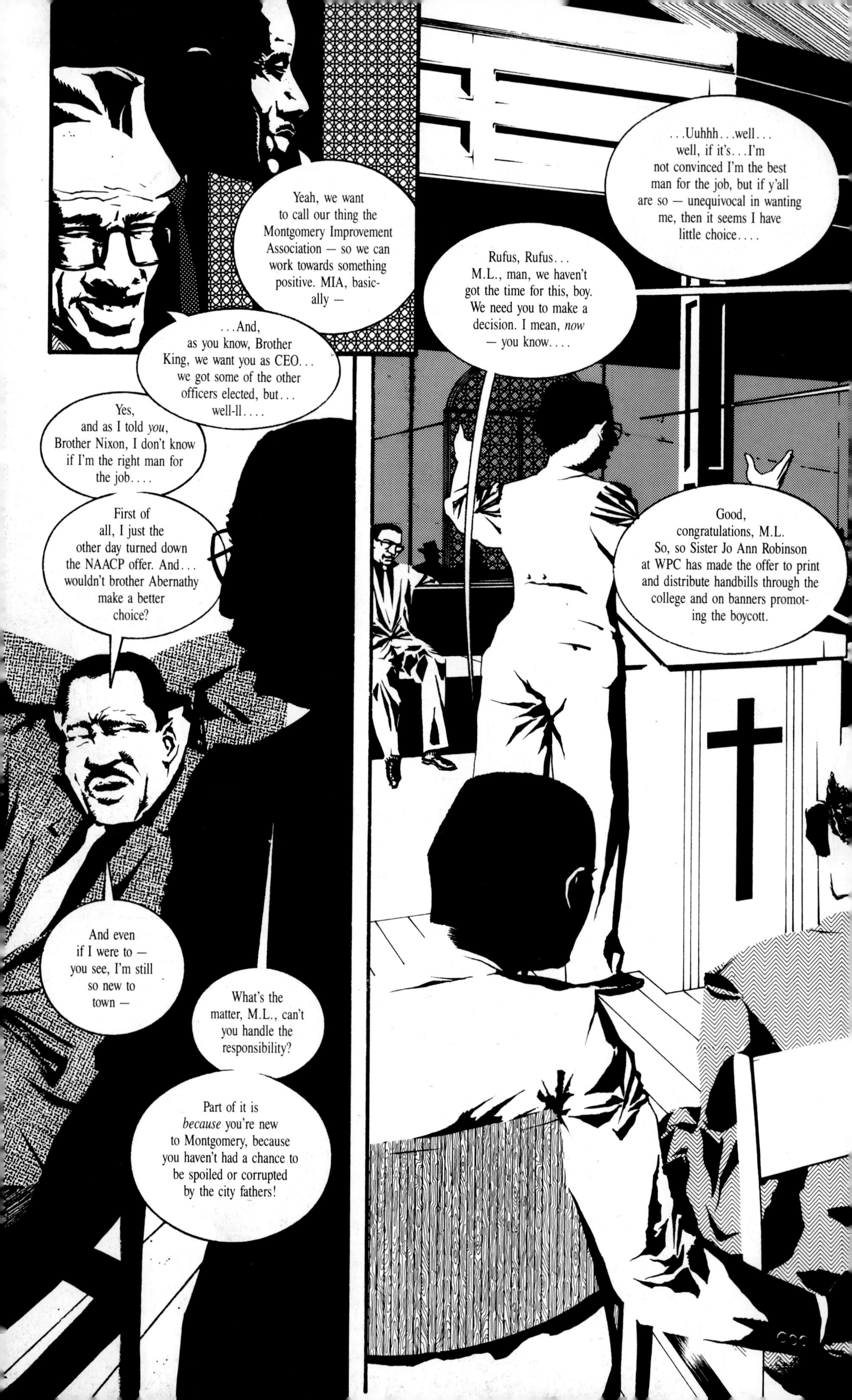
Yeah, we want to call our thing the Montgomery Improvement Association — so we can work towards something positive. MIA, basic-ally —
...And, as you know, Brother King, we want you as CEO... we got some of the other officers elected, but... well-ll....
Yes, and as I told *you*, Brother Nixon, I don't know if I'm the right man for the job....
First of all, I just the other day turned down the NAACP offer. And... wouldn't brother Abernathy make a better choice?
And even if I were to — you see, I'm still so new to town —
What's the matter, M.L., can't you handle the responsibility?
Part of it is *because* you're new to Montgomery, because you haven't had a chance to be spoiled or corrupted by the city fathers!
Rufus, Rufus... M.L., man, we haven't got the time for this, boy. We need you to make a decision. I mean, *now* — you know....
...Uuhhh...well... well, if it's...I'm not convinced I'm the best man for the job, but if y'all are so — unequivocal in wanting me, then it seems I have little choice....
Good, congratulations, M.L. So, so Sister Jo Ann Robinson at WPC has made the offer to print and distribute handbills through the college and on banners promot-ing the boycott.

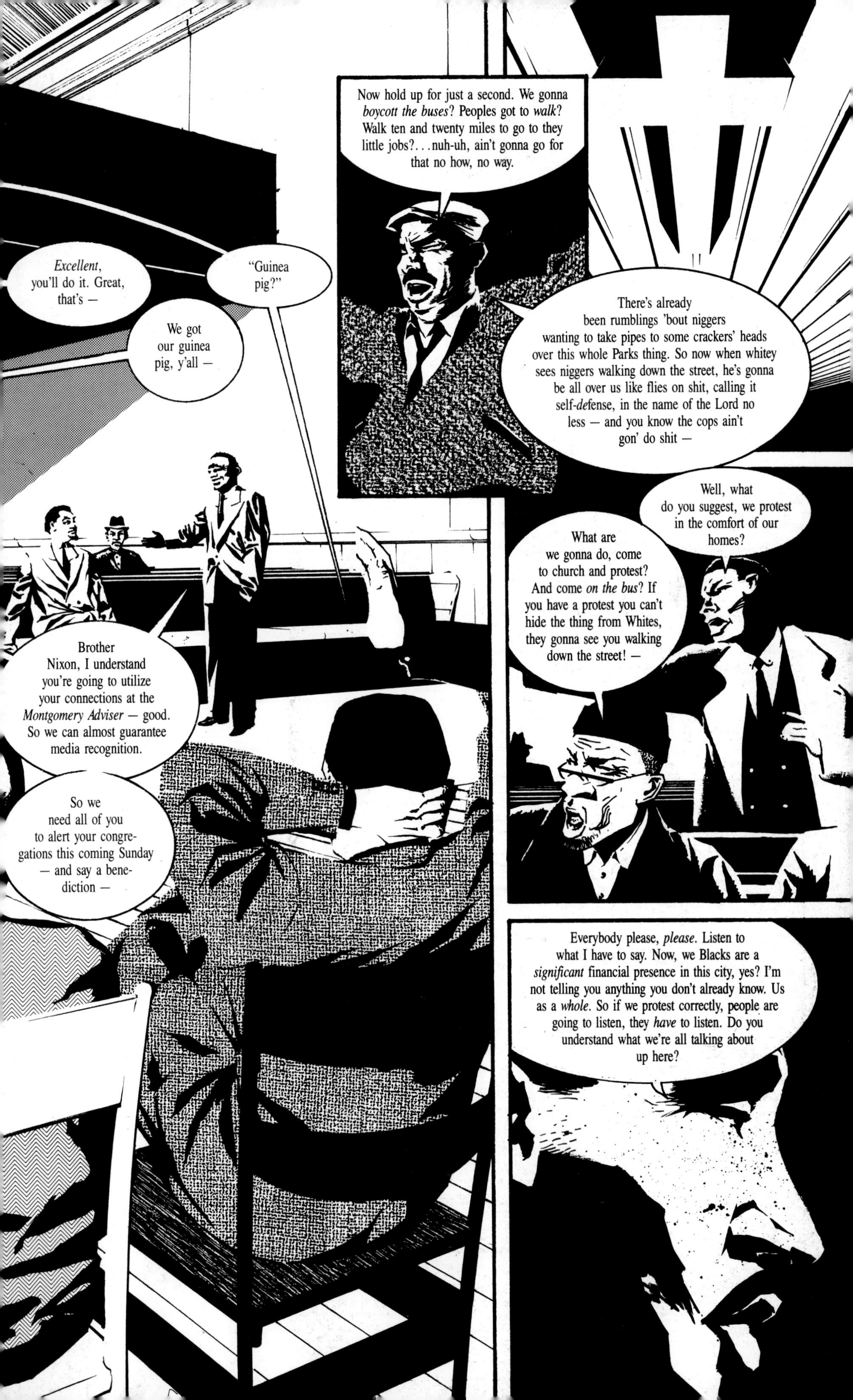
Excellent, you'll do it. Great, that's —
We got our guinea pig, y'all —
"Guinea pig?"
Now hold up for just a second. We gonna boycott the buses? Peoples got to walk? Walk ten and twenty miles to go to they little jobs?. . .nuh-uh, ain't gonna go for that no how, no way.
There's already been rumblings 'bout niggers wanting to take pipes to some crackers' heads over this whole Parks thing. So now when whitey sees niggers walking down the street, he's gonna be all over us like flies on shit, calling it self-defense, in the name of the Lord no less — and you know the cops ain't gon' do shit —
Brother Nixon, I understand you're going to utilize your connections at the Montgomery Adviser — good. So we can almost guarantee media recognition.
So we need all of you to alert your congregations this coming Sunday — and say a benediction —
Well, what do you suggest, we protest in the comfort of our homes?
What are we gonna do, come to church and protest? And come on the bus? If you have a protest you can't hide the thing from Whites, they gonna see you walking down the street! —
Everybody please, please. Listen to what I have to say. Now, we Blacks are a significant financial presence in this city, yes? I'm not telling you anything you don't already know. Us as a whole. So if we protest correctly, people are going to listen, they have to listen. Do you understand what we're all talking about up here?

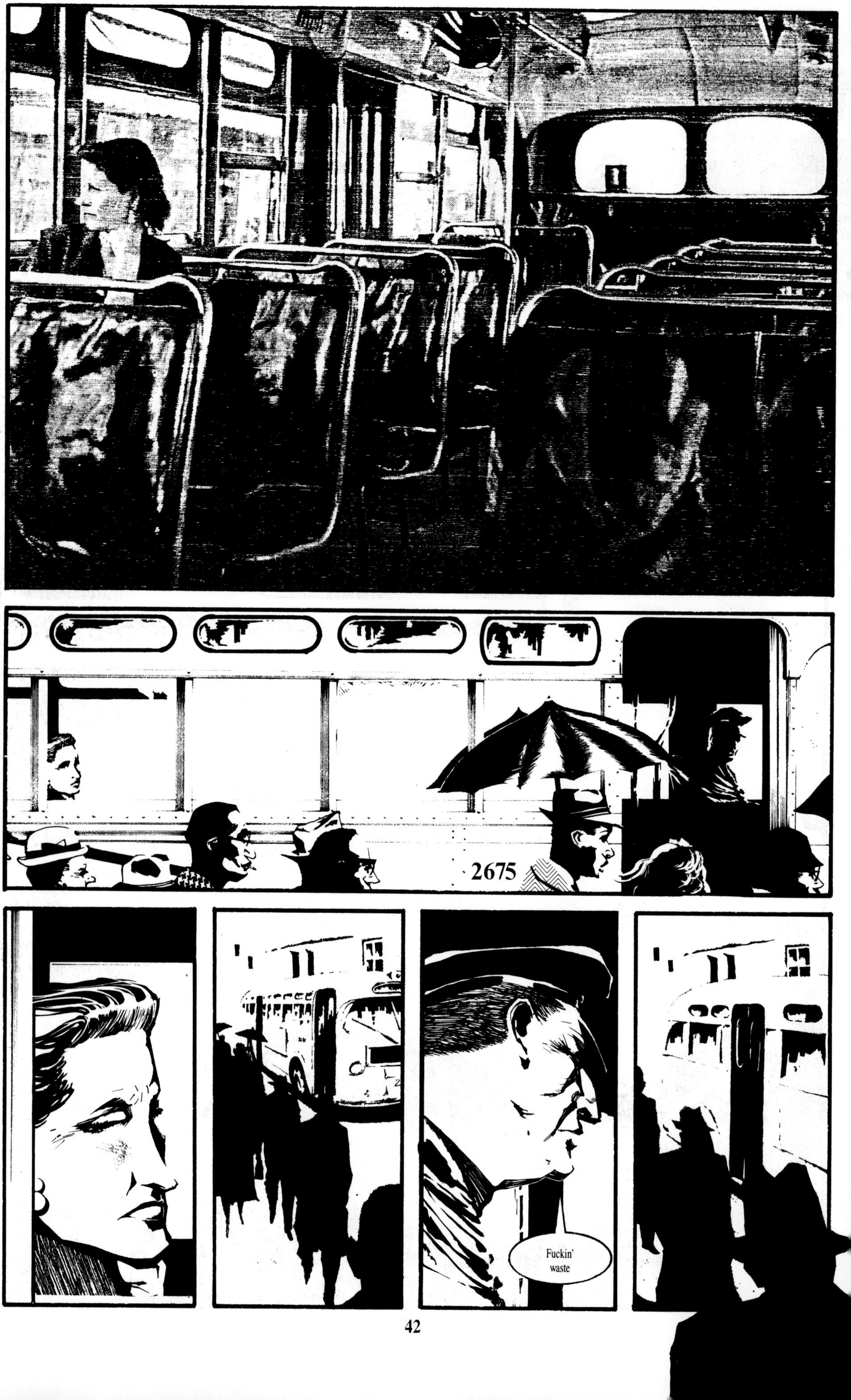
2675
Fuckin'
waste

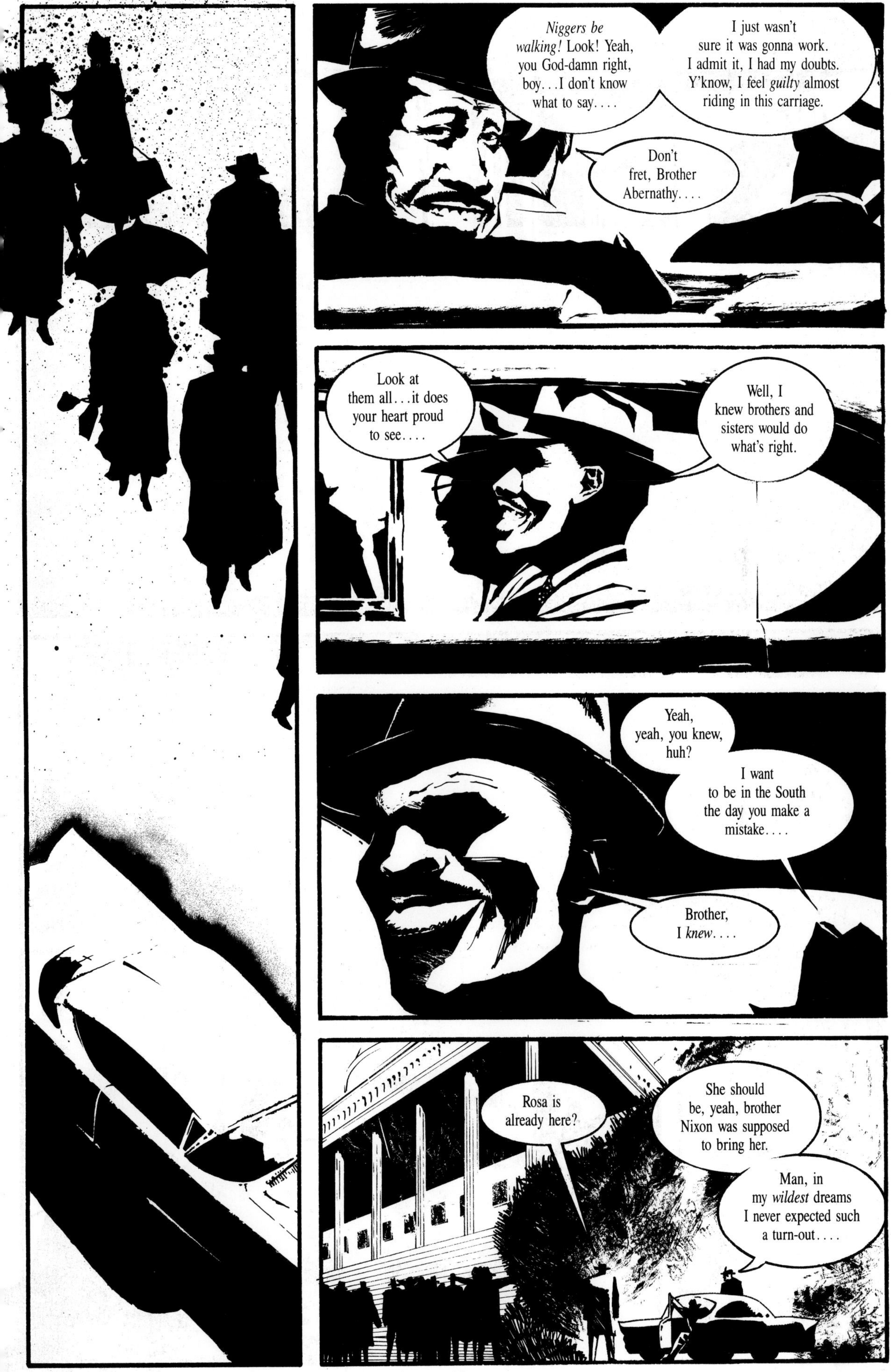
Niggers be walking! Look! Yeah, you God-damn right, boy. . . I don't know what to say. . . .
I just wasn't sure it was gonna work. I admit it, I had my doubts. Y'know, I feel *guilty* almost riding in this carriage.
Don't fret, Brother Abernathy. . . .
Look at them all. . . it does your heart proud to see. . . .
Well, I knew brothers and sisters would do what's right.
Yeah, yeah, you knew, huh?
I want to be in the South the day you make a mistake. . . .
Brother, I *knew*. . . .
Rosa is already here?
She should be, yeah, brother Nixon was supposed to bring her.
Man, in my *wildest* dreams I never expected such a turn-out. . . .

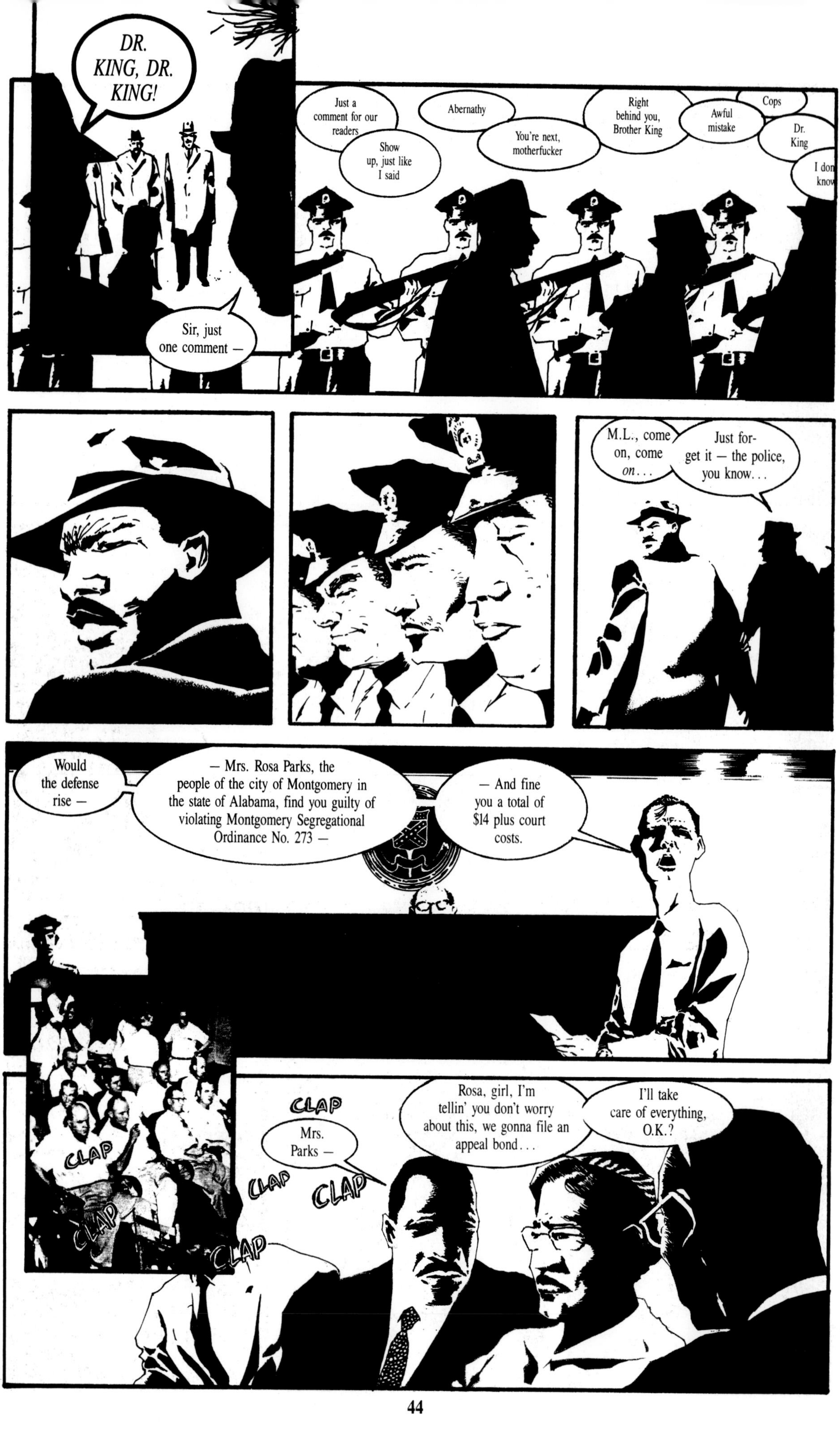
DR. KING, DR. KING!
Just a comment for our readers
Show up, just like I said
Abernathy
You're next, motherfucker
Right behind you, Brother King
Awful mistake
Cops
Dr. King
Sir, just one comment —
M.L., come on, come *on*...
Just forget it — the police, you know...
Would the defense rise —
— Mrs. Rosa Parks, the people of the city of Montgomery in the state of Alabama, find you guilty of violating Montgomery Segregational Ordinance No. 273 —
— And fine you a total of $14 plus court costs.
CLAP
Mrs. Parks —
Rosa, girl, I'm tellin' you don't worry about this, we gonna file an appeal bond...
I'll take care of everything, O.K.?
CLAP
CLAP
CLAP
CLAP
CLAP

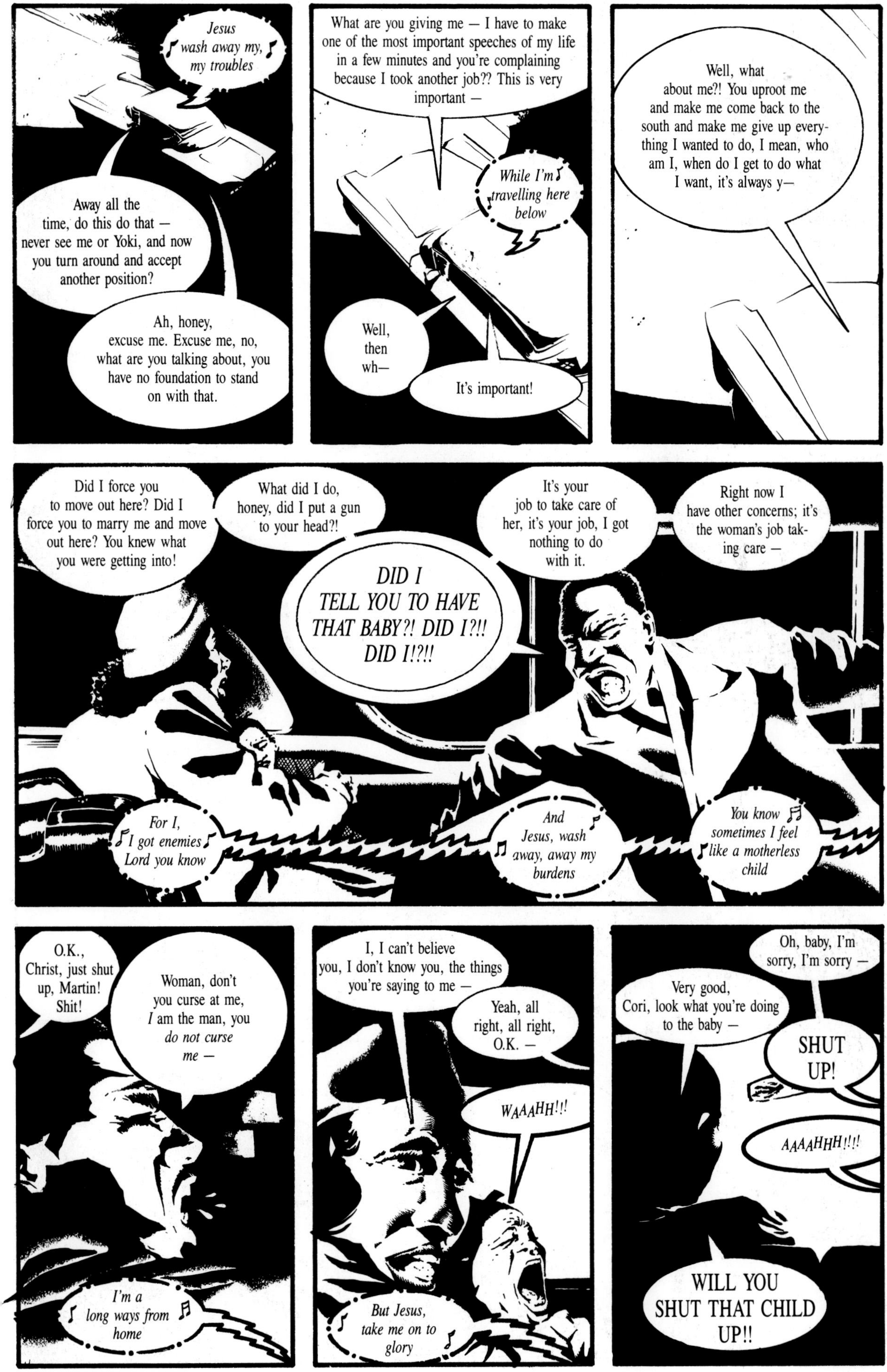
Jesus wash away my, my troubles
Away all the time, do this do that — never see me or Yoki, and now you turn around and accept another position?
Ah, honey, excuse me. Excuse me, no, what are you talking about, you have no foundation to stand on with that.
What are you giving me — I have to make one of the most important speeches of my life in a few minutes and you're complaining because I took another job?? This is very important —
While I'm travelling here below
Well, then wh—
It's important!
Well, what about me?! You uproot me and make me come back to the south and make me give up everything I wanted to do, I mean, who am I, when do I get to do what I want, it's always y—
Did I force you to move out here? Did I force you to marry me and move out here? You knew what you were getting into!
What did I do, honey, did I put a gun to your head?!
DID I TELL YOU TO HAVE THAT BABY?! DID I?!! DID I!?!!
It's your job to take care of her, it's your job, I got nothing to do with it.
Right now I have other concerns; it's the woman's job taking care —
For I, I got enemies Lord you know
And Jesus, wash away, away my burdens
You know sometimes I feel like a motherless child
O.K., Christ, just shut up, Martin! Shit!
Woman, don't you curse at me, I am the man, you do not curse me —
I'm a long ways from home
I, I can't believe you, I don't know you, the things you're saying to me —
Yeah, all right, all right, O.K. —
WAAAHH!!!
But Jesus, take me on to glory
Oh, baby, I'm sorry, I'm sorry —
Very good, Cori, look what you're doing to the baby —
SHUT UP!
AAAAHHH!!!!
WILL YOU SHUT THAT CHILD UP!!

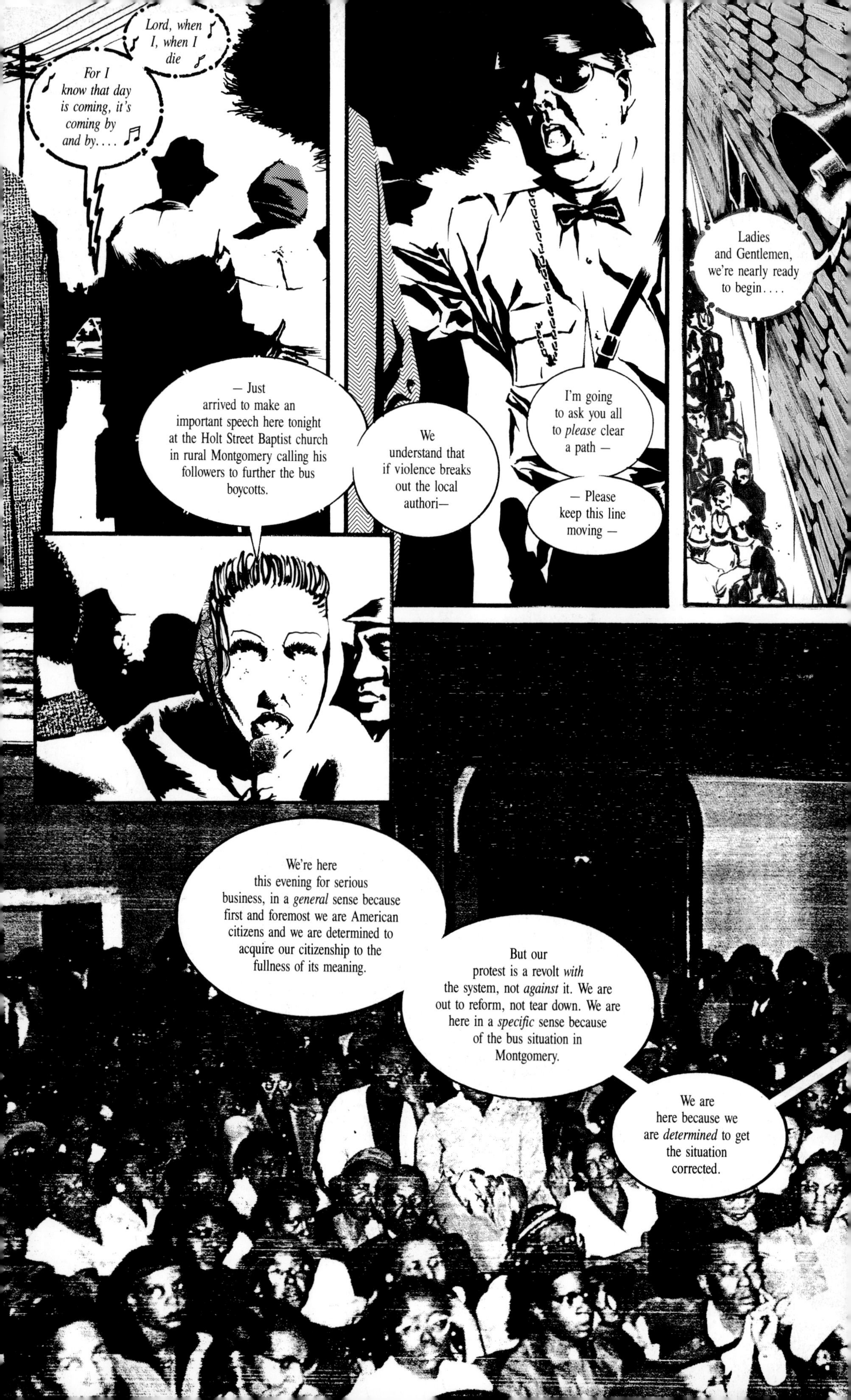
For I know that day is coming, it's coming by and by....
Lord, when I, when I die
I'm going to ask you all to please clear a path —
— Please keep this line moving —
Ladies and Gentlemen, we're nearly ready to begin....
— Just arrived to make an important speech here tonight at the Holt Street Baptist church in rural Montgomery calling his followers to further the bus boycotts.
We understand that if violence breaks out the local authori—
We're here this evening for serious business, in a general sense because first and foremost we are American citizens and we are determined to acquire our citizenship to the fullness of its meaning.
But our protest is a revolt with the system, not against it. We are out to reform, not tear down. We are here in a specific sense because of the bus situation in Montgomery.
We are here because we are determined to get the situation corrected.

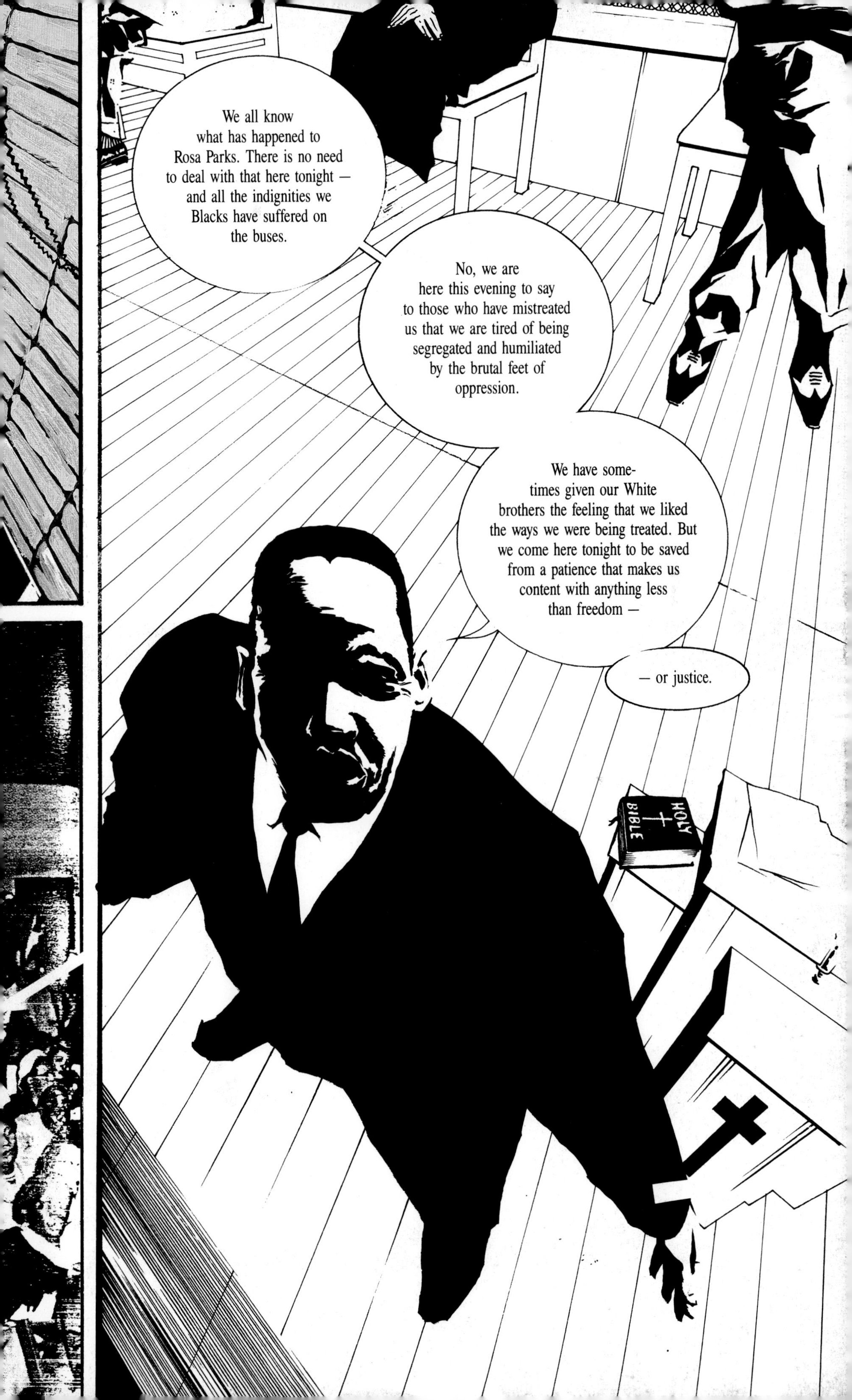

We all know what has happened to Rosa Parks. There is no need to deal with that here tonight — and all the indignities we Blacks have suffered on the buses.
No, we are here this evening to say to those who have mistreated us that we are tired of being segregated and humiliated by the brutal feet of oppression.
We have sometimes given our White brothers the feeling that we liked the ways we were being treated. But we come here tonight to be saved from a patience that makes us content with anything less than freedom —
— or justice.
HOLY BIBLE

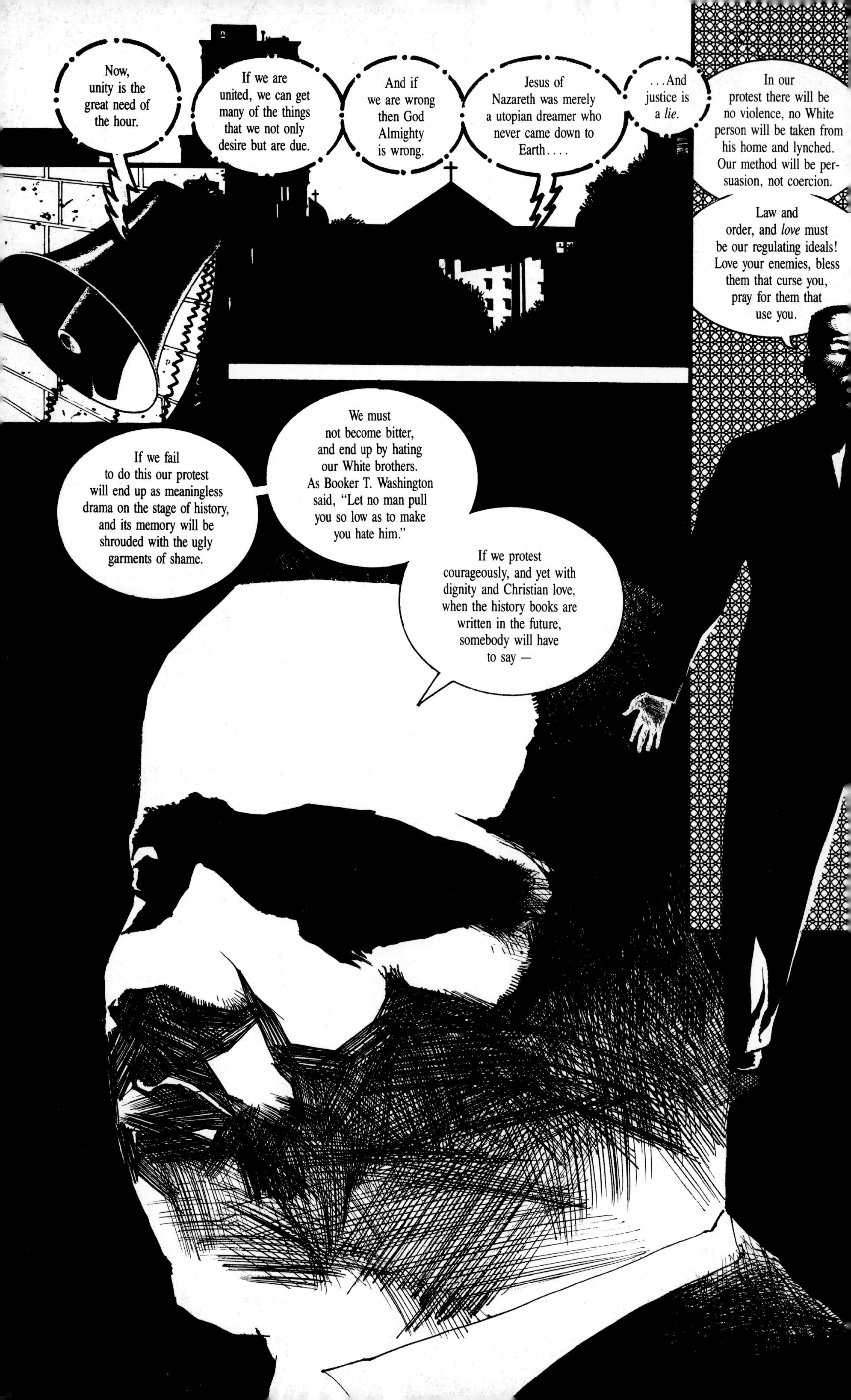
Now, unity is the great need of the hour.
If we are united, we can get many of the things that we not only desire but are due.
And if we are wrong then God Almighty is wrong.
Jesus of Nazareth was merely a utopian dreamer who never came down to Earth. . . .
. . .And justice is a *lie*.
In our protest there will be no violence, no White person will be taken from his home and lynched. Our method will be persuasion, not coercion.
Law and order, and *love* must be our regulating ideals! Love your enemies, bless them that curse you, pray for them that use you.
If we fail to do this our protest will end up as meaningless drama on the stage of history, and its memory will be shrouded with the ugly garments of shame.
We must not become bitter, and end up by hating our White brothers. As Booker T. Washington said, "Let no man pull you so low as to make you hate him."
If we protest courageously, and yet with dignity and Christian love, when the history books are written in the future, somebody will have to say —

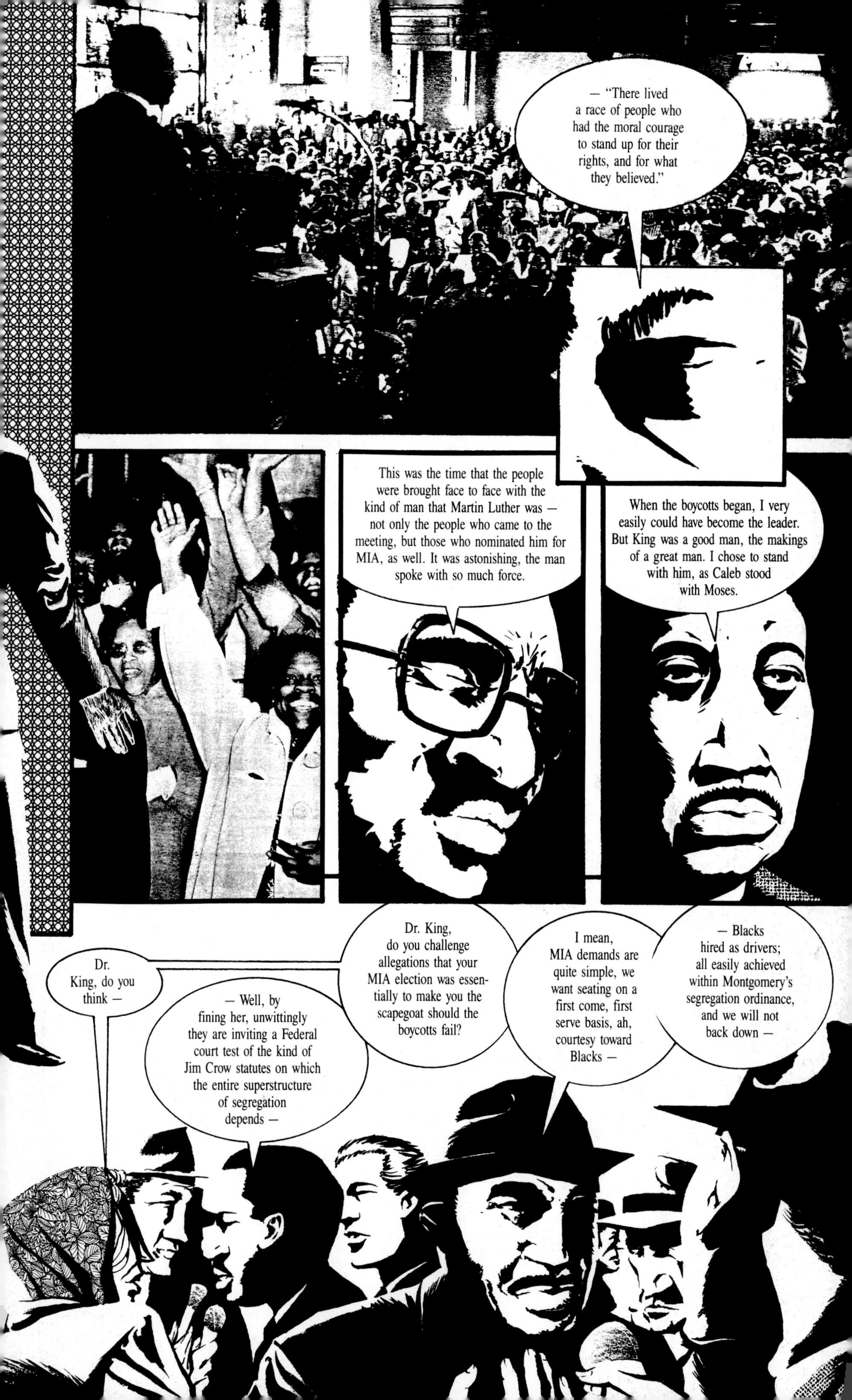
— "There lived a race of people who had the moral courage to stand up for their rights, and for what they believed."
This was the time that the people were brought face to face with the kind of man that Martin Luther was — not only the people who came to the meeting, but those who nominated him for MIA, as well. It was astonishing, the man spoke with so much force.
When the boycotts began, I very easily could have become the leader. But King was a good man, the makings of a great man. I chose to stand with him, as Caleb stood with Moses.
Dr. King, do you think —
— Well, by fining her, unwittingly they are inviting a Federal court test of the kind of Jim Crow statutes on which the entire superstructure of segregation depends —
Dr. King, do you challenge allegations that your MIA election was essentially to make you the scapegoat should the boycotts fail?
I mean, MIA demands are quite simple, we want seating on a first come, first serve basis, ah, courtesy toward Blacks —
— Blacks hired as drivers; all easily achieved within Montgomery's segregation ordinance, and we will not back down —

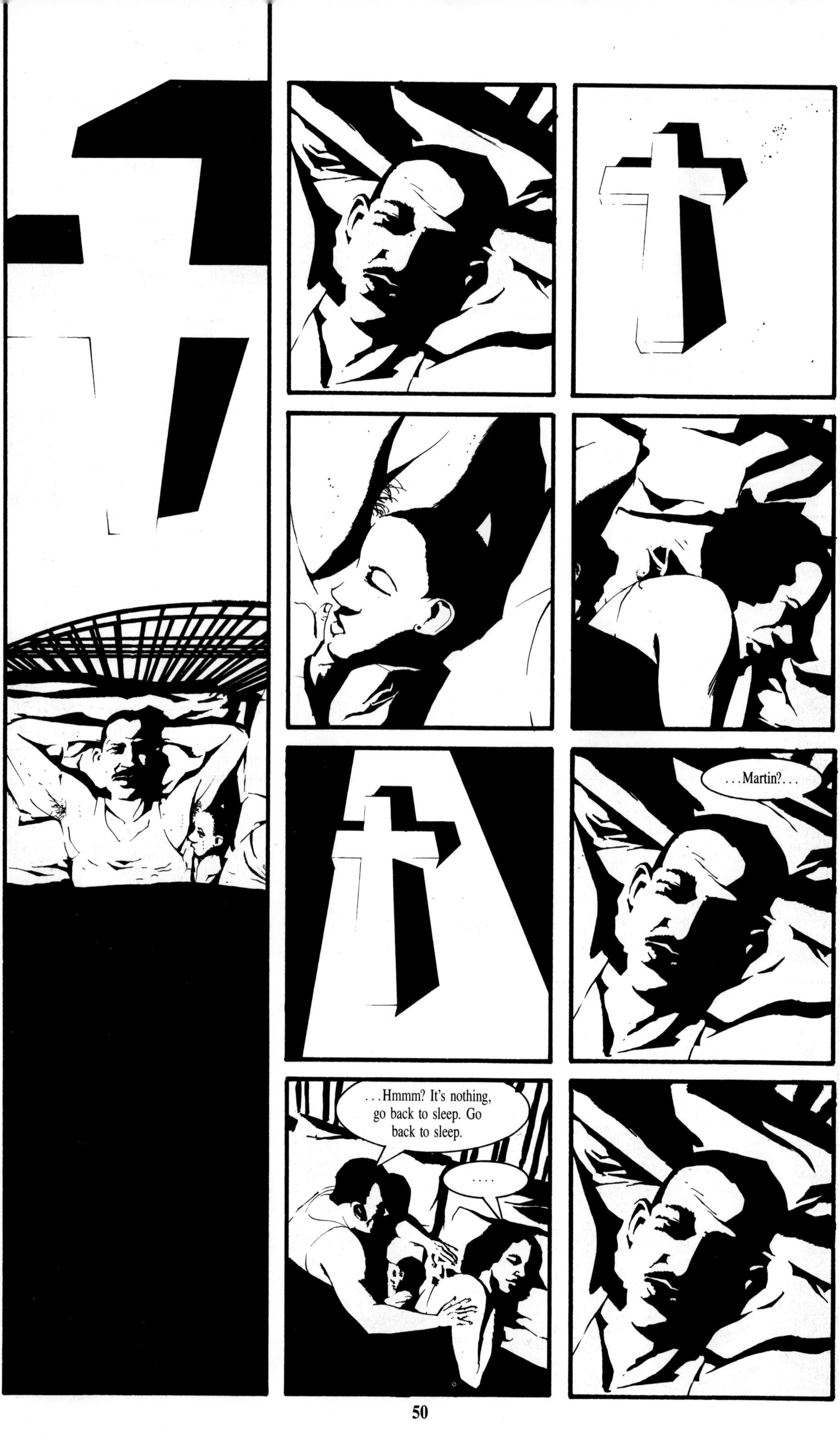
. . . Martin?. . .
. . . Hmmm? It's nothing, go back to sleep. Go back to sleep.
. . . .

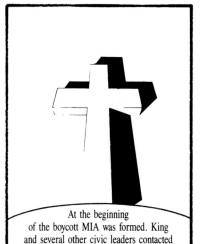

At the beginning of the boycott MIA was formed. King and several other civic leaders contacted Montgomery's eight Black-owned taxi companies, operating with a combined fleet of 60 to 70 cars, and persuaded them to haul Black people for a few cents apiece.

But to try to force us back into the buses, the police commissioner eventually ordered the taxis to charge the legal minimum rate of forty-five cents per customer, thus ending cheap fares for the boycotters.

That was the start of the MIA devised carpools. It was funny, you'd see cars just, just spilling over onto the street with colored folk. I have a funny memory of people hanging onto the roof of taxis that were too full to get into. But I probably remember wrong.

It was based on the earlier Baton Rouge boycott. They operated out of 48 dispatch and 42 pickup stations established in key sections of the city. Think about that. And all on a volunteer basis. One of the most efficient transportation systems Montgomery ever had.

In those days I worked as a housekeeper. One day my mistress turn at me, she say, "Isn't this bus boycott terrible?" And I said, "Yes, Ma'am, it sure is. And I just told all my young'uns that this kind of thing is White folks' business and we just stay off the buses 'til they get it settled."

Actually, there were a great many Whites that were sympathetic to our cause. I know of one story where a Negro domestic grew tired of the boycott and returned to the buses. Well, when her White employer found this out she fired her, saying, "If you have no race pride — if your own people can't trust you — then I can't trust you in my house."

Altogether the boycott dragged on for a little over a year. Many of us Blacks were getting good and fed up because nothing seemed to be happening. Just day after day of walking, walking, walking. By this time, Whites were resorting to psychological warfare to break the boycotts.

Dr. King was receiving 30 to 40 hate letters and death threats a day. We were mad. We wanted to take some Whites *out*. But Dr. King was adamant about this being a non-violent protest, and he practiced what he preached. On January 30 of '56, King's house was bombed.

No one was hurt, but the people were up in arms, we wanted blood. There was nearly a riot, but Dr. King said to let-it-go. A lot of people couldn't understand him.

A couple of meetings between a special MIA deputation and the city fathers took place in the commissioner's chambers at City Hall to get MIA demands met. But Mayor Gayle laughed at us; nothing was done.

He didn't take the boycott seriously because it was organized by niggers, and there were charges of communist sympathies in Martin's camp, which was not true. Everyone wanted the boycott done with and forgotten, White and Black. ...We owed it to ourselves to continue, you understand?

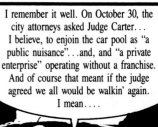

I remember it well. On October 30, the city attorneys asked Judge Carter... I believe, to enjoin the car pool as "a public nuisance"...and, and "a private enterprise" operating without a franchise. And of course that meant if the judge agreed we all would be walkin' again. I mean....

And so, Your Honor, it is the prosecution's position that the car pools be ordered shut down effective immediately—

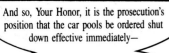

—And that Dr. King be ordered to pay $15,000 in damages for the Montgomery boycott of 1956, ahh, in lost revenues, damages—

Yes. Yes, that's all been covered before, Councellor. Does the defense understand the charges brought before it?

Ahh yes, nolo contendere, your honor—

I just... This, this is it... There's no way....

Martin....

All that work we did...all our work, sacrifice ..for what? For what?

I mean, there is not even any, any doubt — he's not — the judge finding in my favor?...

...There's no way it.... It's, it's — I —

Well, then, there is always... No, when we go back inside, the judge, he —

HEY! DR. KING! DR. KING!

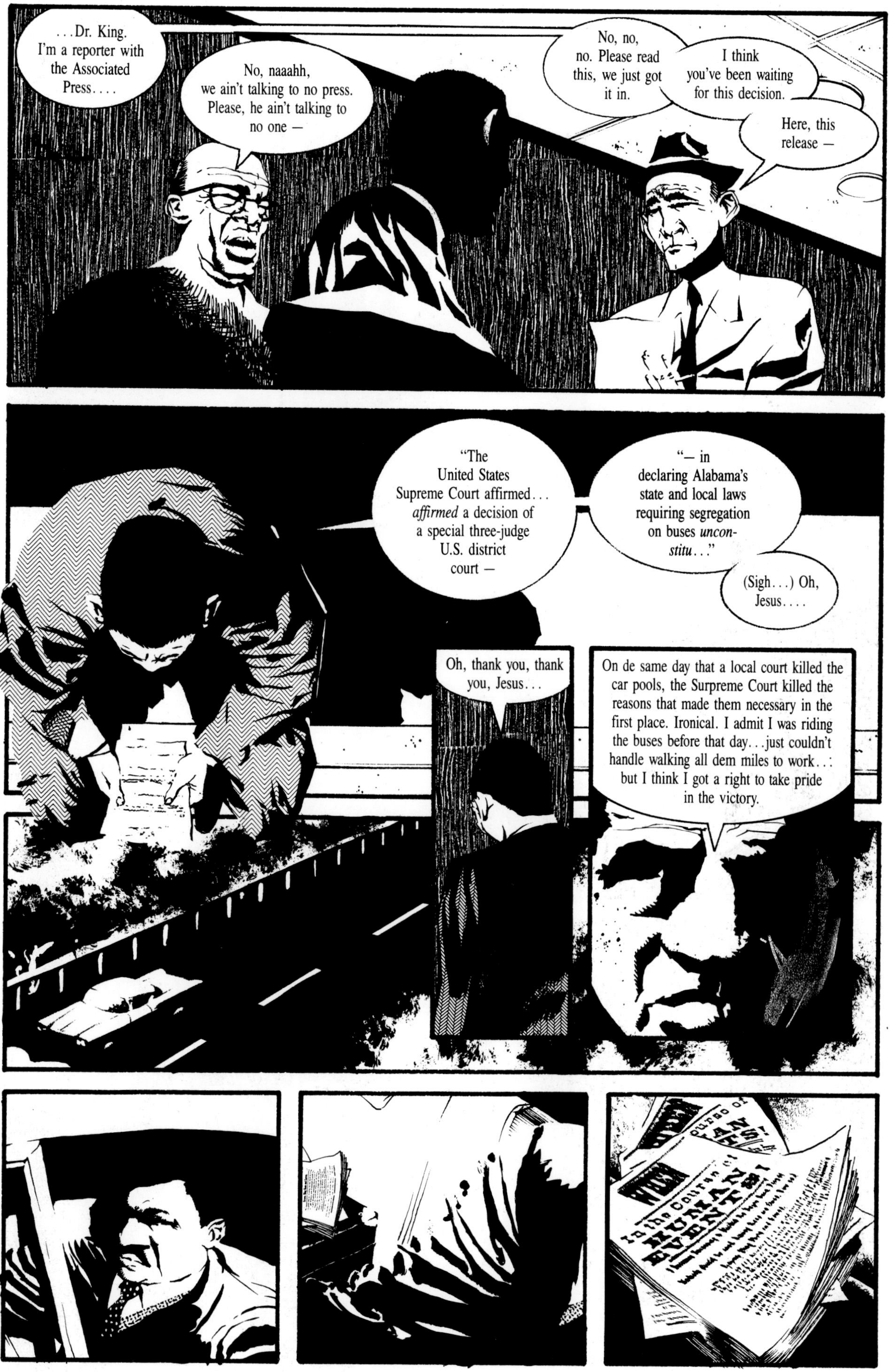
...Dr. King. I'm a reporter with the Associated Press....
No, naaahh, we ain't talking to no press. Please, he ain't talking to no one –
No, no, no. Please read this, we just got it in.
I think you've been waiting for this decision.
Here, this release –
"The United States Supreme Court affirmed... *affirmed* a decision of a special three-judge U.S. district court –
"– in declaring Alabama's state and local laws requiring segregation on buses *uncon-stitu*..."
(Sigh...) Oh, Jesus....
Oh, thank you, thank you, Jesus...
On de same day that a local court killed the car pools, the Surpreme Court killed the reasons that made them necessary in the first place. Ironical. I admit I was riding the buses before that day...just couldn't handle walking all dem miles to work...: but I think I got a right to take pride in the victory.

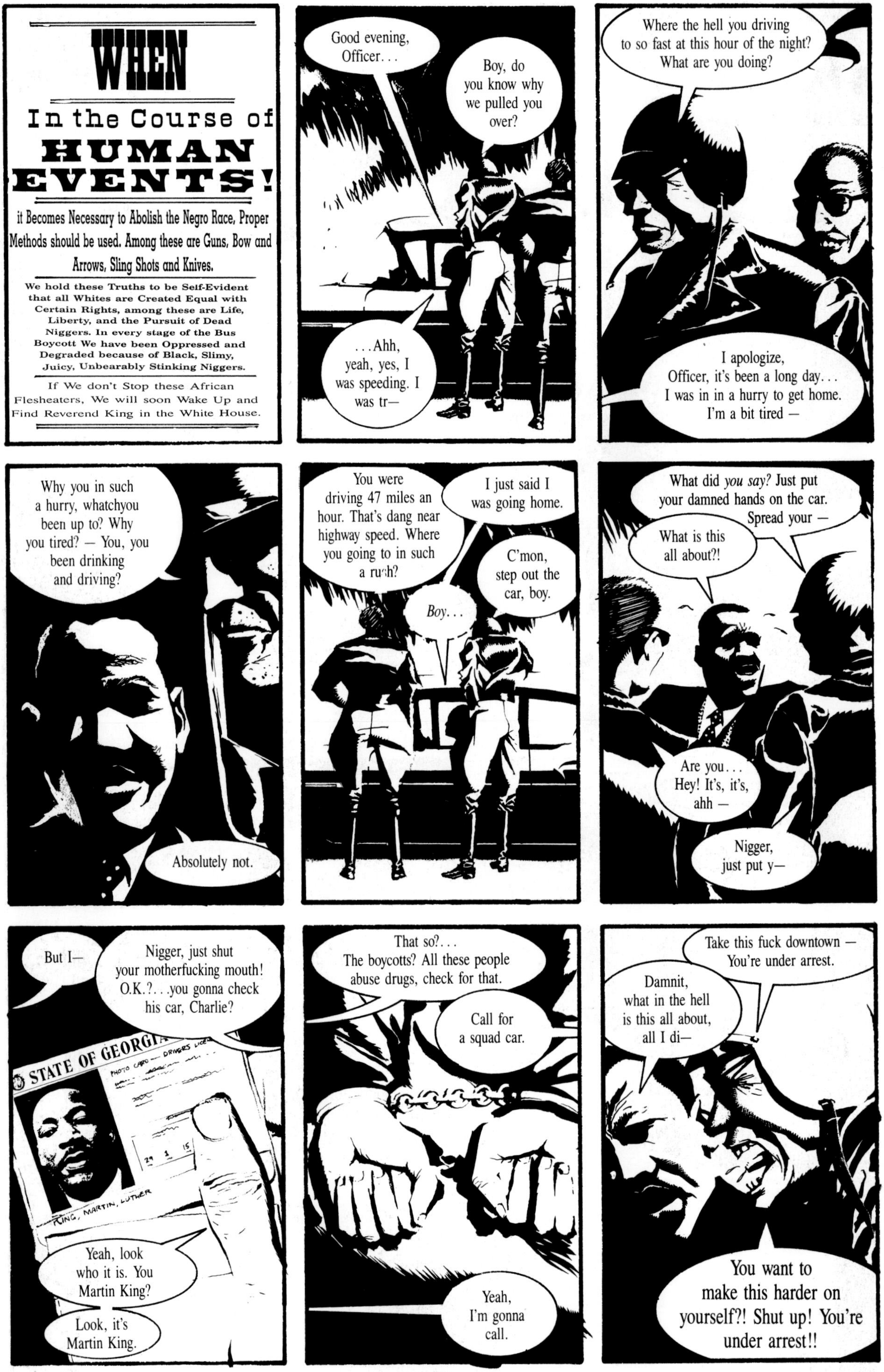
WHEN
In the Course of
HUMAN EVENTS!
it Becomes Necessary to Abolish the Negro Race, Proper Methods should be used. Among these are Guns, Bow and Arrows, Sling Shots and Knives.
We hold these Truths to be Self-Evident that all Whites are Created Equal with Certain Rights, among these are Life, Liberty, and the Pursuit of Dead Niggers. In every stage of the Bus Boycott We have been Oppressed and Degraded because of Black, Slimy, Juicy, Unbearably Stinking Niggers.
If We don't Stop these African Flesheaters, We will soon Wake Up and Find Reverend King in the White House.
Good evening, Officer. . .
Boy, do you know why we pulled you over?
. . .Ahh, yeah, yes, I was speeding. I was tr—
Where the hell you driving to so fast at this hour of the night? What are you doing?
I apologize, Officer, it's been a long day. . . I was in in a hurry to get home. I'm a bit tired —
Why you in such a hurry, whatchyou been up to? Why you tired? — You, you been drinking and driving?
Absolutely not.
You were driving 47 miles an hour. That's dang near highway speed. Where you going to in such a rush?
I just said I was going home.
C'mon, step out the car, boy.
Boy. . .
What did *you say?* Just put your damned hands on the car. Spread your —
What is this all about?!
Are you. . . Hey! It's, it's, ahh —
Nigger, just put y—
But I—
Nigger, just shut your motherfucking mouth! O.K.?. . .you gonna check his car, Charlie?
STATE OF GEORGIA
KING, MARTIN, LUTHER
Yeah, look who it is. You Martin King?
Look, it's Martin King.
That so?. . . The boycotts? All these people abuse drugs, check for that.
Call for a squad car.
Yeah, I'm gonna call.
Take this fuck downtown — You're under arrest.
Damnit, what in the hell is this all about, all I di—
You want to make this harder on yourself?! Shut up! You're under arrest!!

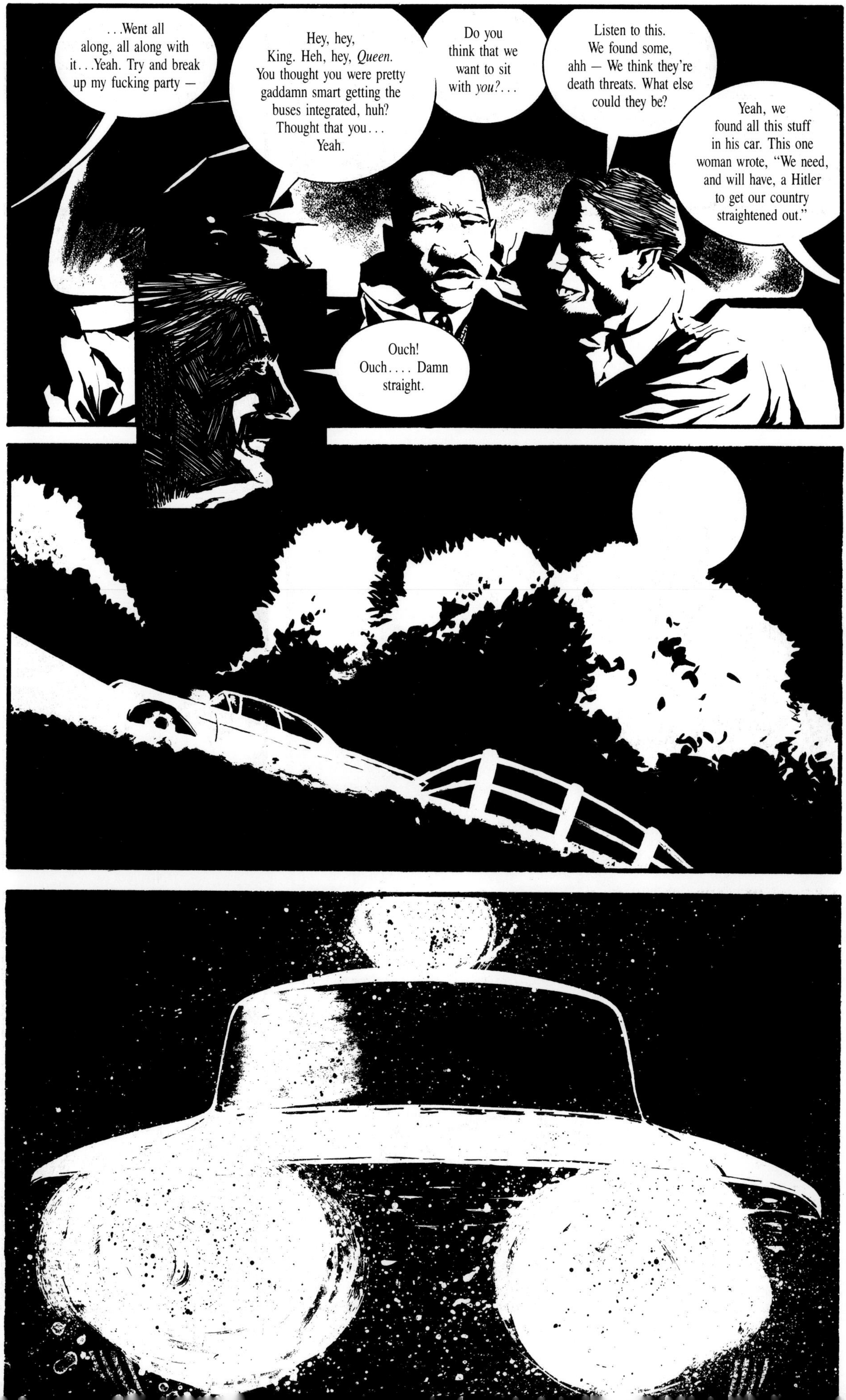
...Went all along, all along with it...Yeah. Try and break up my fucking party —
Hey, hey, King. Heh, hey, *Queen.* You thought you were pretty gaddamn smart getting the buses integrated, huh? Thought that you... Yeah.
Do you think that we want to sit with *you?*...
Listen to this. We found some, ahh — We think they're death threats. What else could they be?
Yeah, we found all this stuff in his car. This one woman wrote, "We need, and will have, a Hitler to get our country straightened out."
Ouch! Ouch.... Damn straight.

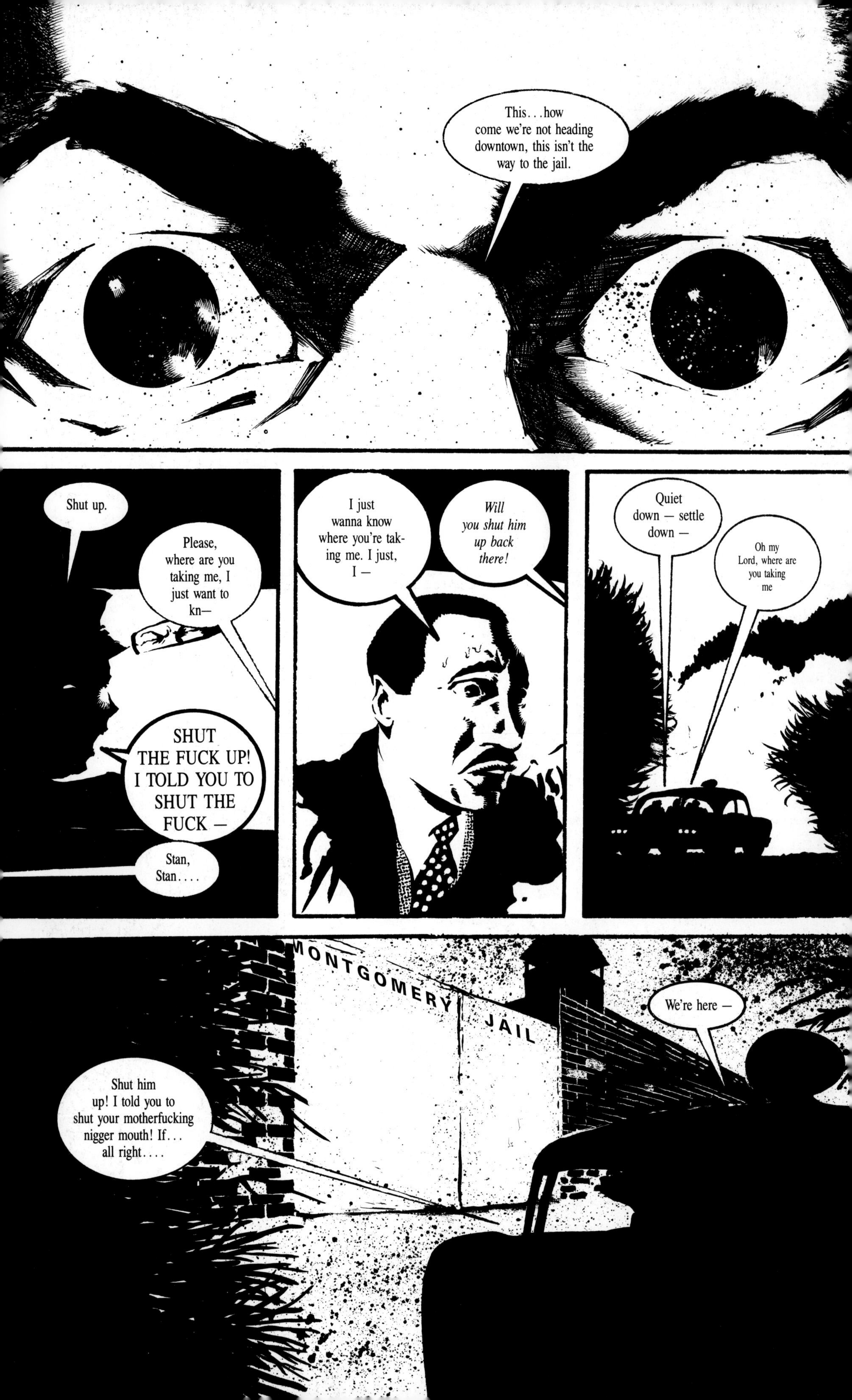
This. . .how come we're not heading downtown, this isn't the way to the jail.
Shut up.
Please, where are you taking me, I just want to kn—
SHUT THE FUCK UP! I TOLD YOU TO SHUT THE FUCK —
Stan, Stan. . . .
I just wanna know where you're tak-ing me. I just, I —
Will you shut him up back there!
Quiet down — settle down —
Oh my Lord, where are you taking me
MONTGOMERY JAIL
We're here —
Shut him up! I told you to shut your motherfucking nigger mouth! If. . . all right. . . .

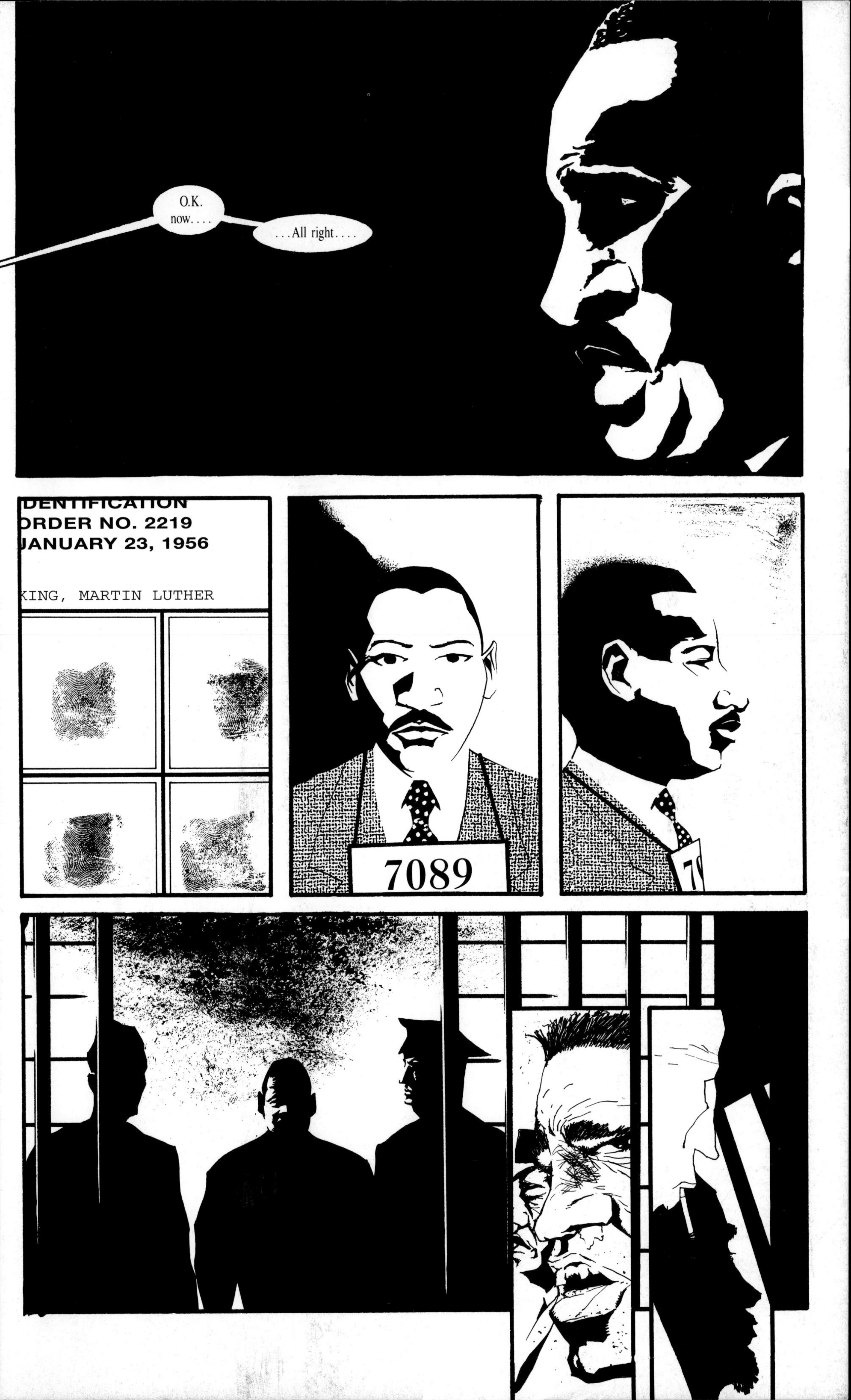
O.K. now. . . .
. . . All right. . . .
DENTIFICATION
ORDER NO. 2219
JANUARY 23, 1956
KING, MARTIN LUTHER
7089

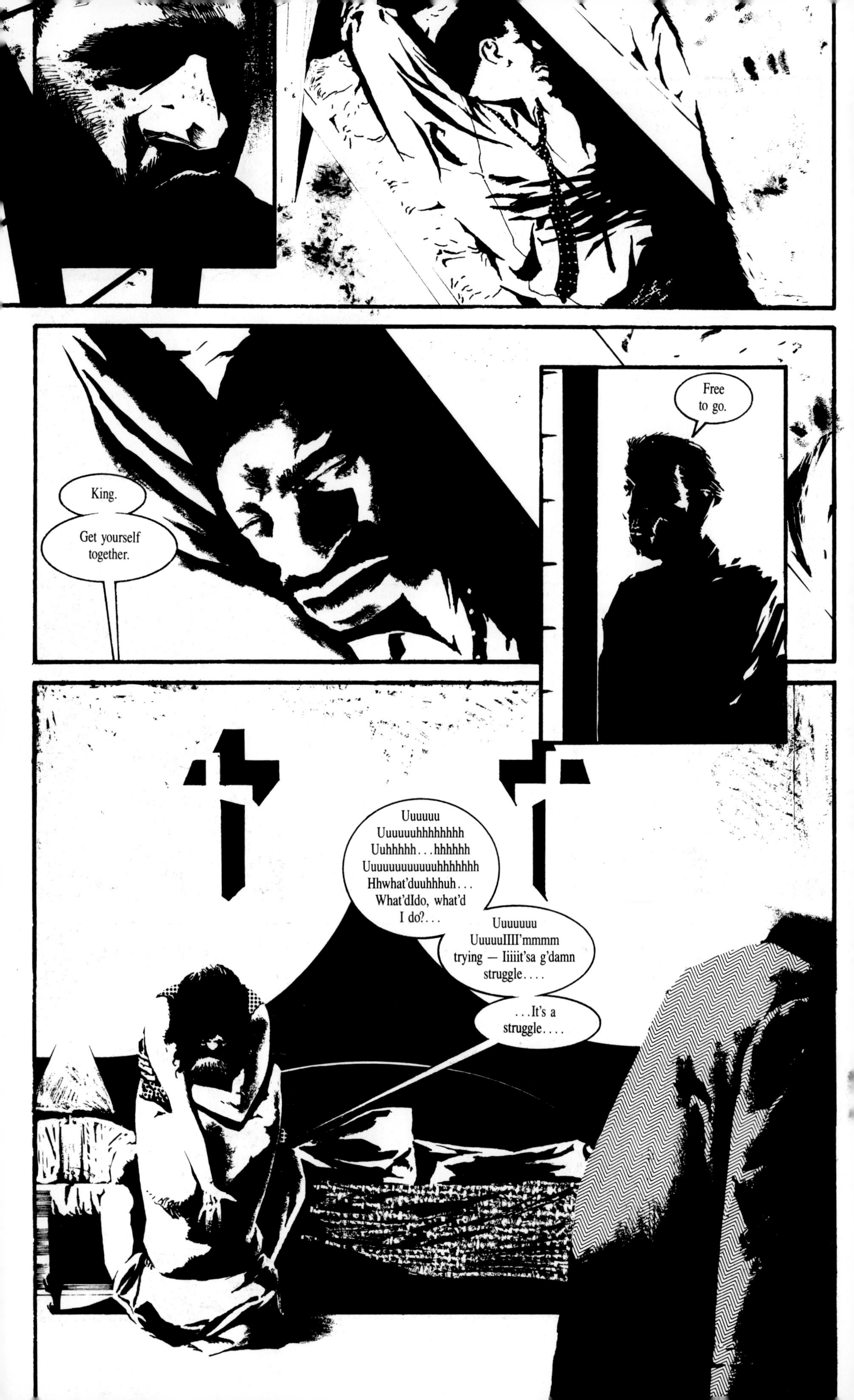
King.
Get yourself together.
Free to go.
Uuuuuu Uuuuuuhhhhhhhh Uuhhhhh. . . hhhhhh Uuuuuuuuuuuuuhhhhhhh Hhwhat'duuhhhuh. . . What'dIdo, what'd I do?. . .
Uuuuuu UuuuuIIII'mmmm trying — Iiiiit'sa g'damn struggle. . . .
. . .It's a struggle. . . .

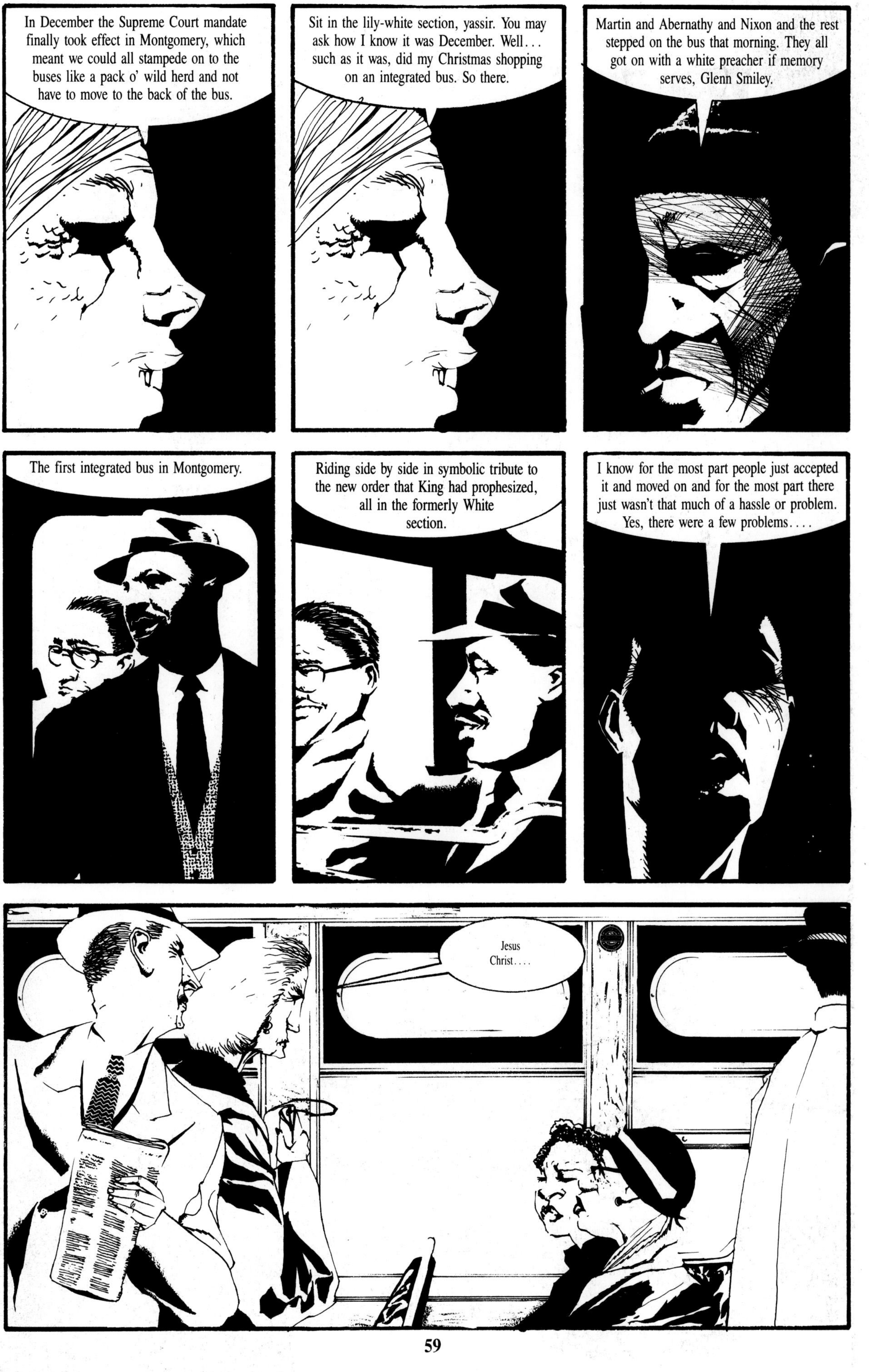
In December the Supreme Court mandate finally took effect in Montgomery, which meant we could all stampede on to the buses like a pack o' wild herd and not have to move to the back of the bus.
Sit in the lily-white section, yassir. You may ask how I know it was December. Well... such as it was, did my Christmas shopping on an integrated bus. So there.
Martin and Abernathy and Nixon and the rest stepped on the bus that morning. They all got on with a white preacher if memory serves, Glenn Smiley.
The first integrated bus in Montgomery.
Riding side by side in symbolic tribute to the new order that King had prophesized, all in the formerly White section.
I know for the most part people just accepted it and moved on and for the most part there just wasn't that much of a hassle or problem. Yes, there were a few problems....
Jesus Christ....

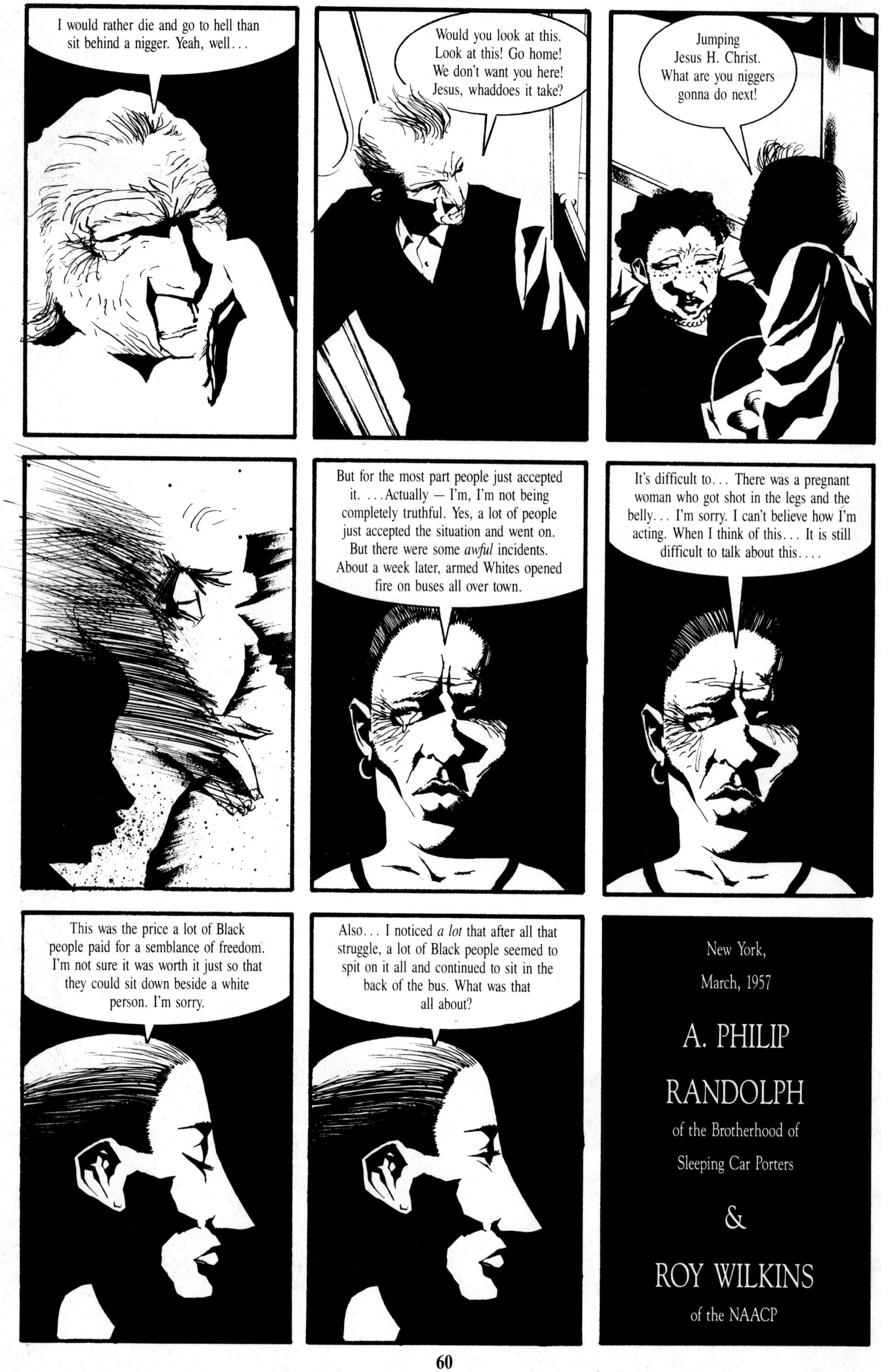
I would rather die and go to hell than sit behind a nigger. Yeah, well...
Would you look at this. Look at this! Go home! We don't want you here! Jesus, whaddoes it take?
Jumping Jesus H. Christ. What are you niggers gonna do next!
But for the most part people just accepted it. ...Actually — I'm, I'm not being completely truthful. Yes, a lot of people just accepted the situation and went on. But there were some *awful* incidents. About a week later, armed Whites opened fire on buses all over town.
It's difficult to... There was a pregnant woman who got shot in the legs and the belly... I'm sorry. I can't believe how I'm acting. When I think of this... It is still difficult to talk about this....
This was the price a lot of Black people paid for a semblance of freedom. I'm not sure it was worth it just so that they could sit down beside a white person. I'm sorry.
Also... I noticed *a lot* that after all that struggle, a lot of Black people seemed to spit on it all and continued to sit in the back of the bus. What was that all about?
New York, March, 1957
A. PHILIP RANDOLPH of the Brotherhood of Sleeping Car Porters & ROY WILKINS of the NAACP

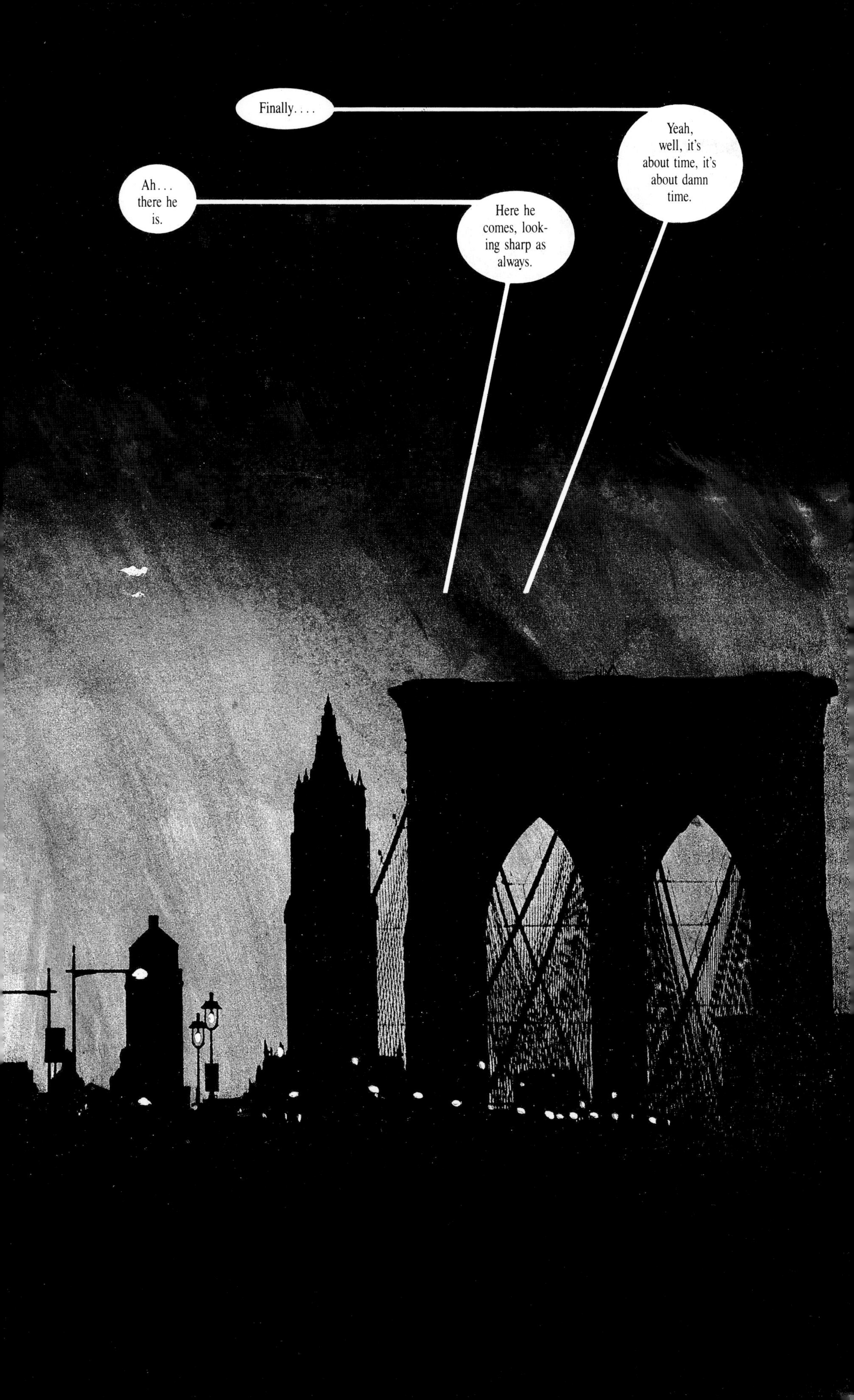
Ah . . . there he is.
Finally. . . .
Here he comes, look-ing sharp as always.
Yeah, well, it's about time, it's about damn time.

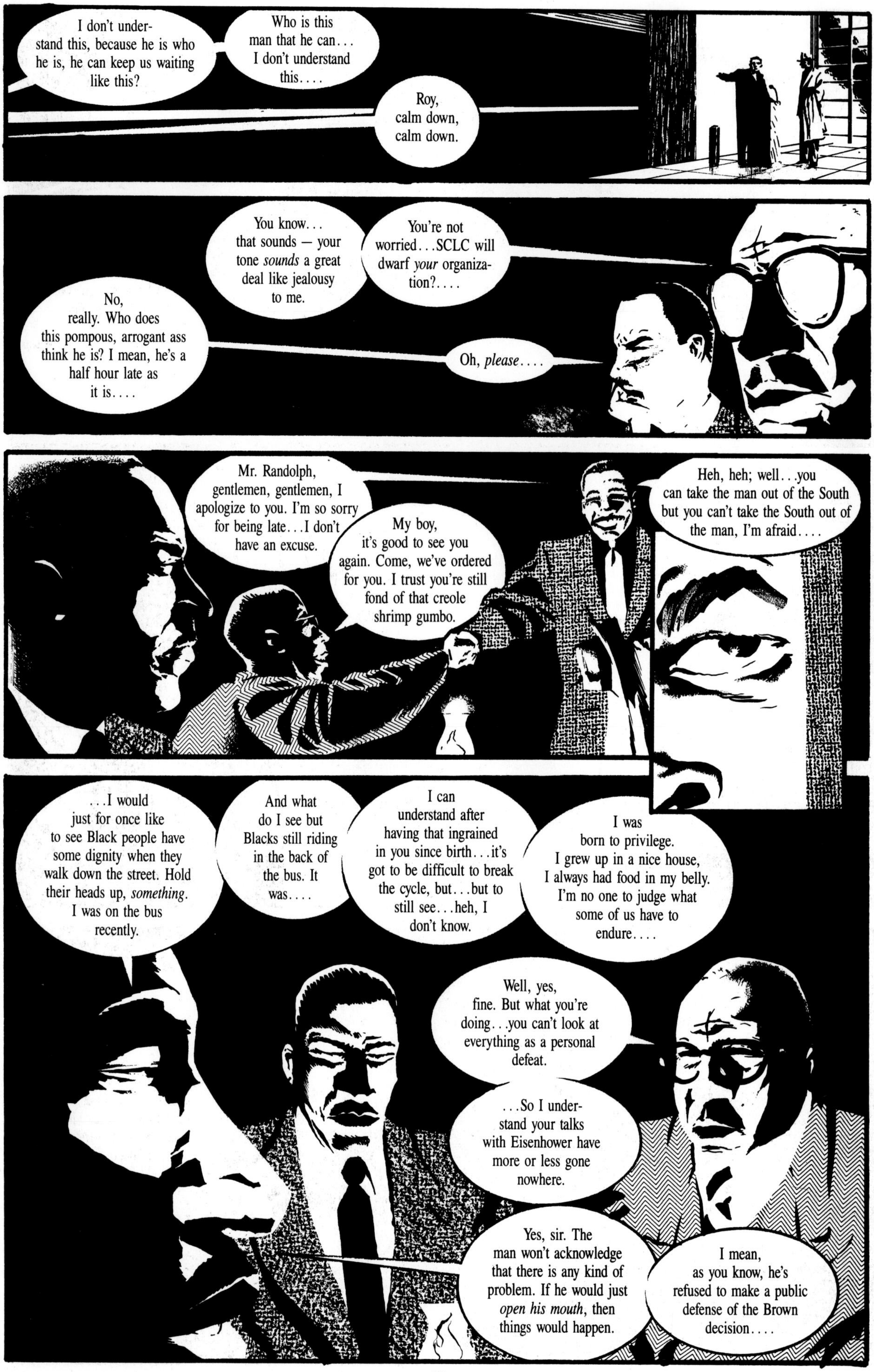
I don't understand this, because he is who he is, he can keep us waiting like this?
Who is this man that he can... I don't understand this....
Roy, calm down, calm down.
You know... that sounds — your tone *sounds* a great deal like jealousy to me.
You're not worried...SCLC will dwarf *your* organization?....
No, really. Who does this pompous, arrogant ass think he is? I mean, he's a half hour late as it is....
Oh, *please*....
Mr. Randolph, gentlemen, gentlemen, I apologize to you. I'm so sorry for being late...I don't have an excuse.
My boy, it's good to see you again. Come, we've ordered for you. I trust you're still fond of that creole shrimp gumbo.
Heh, heh; well...you can take the man out of the South but you can't take the South out of the man, I'm afraid....
...I would just for once like to see Black people have some dignity when they walk down the street. Hold their heads up, *something*. I was on the bus recently.
And what do I see but Blacks still riding in the back of the bus. It was....
I can understand after having that ingrained in you since birth...it's got to be difficult to break the cycle, but...but to still see...heh, I don't know.
I was born to privilege. I grew up in a nice house, I always had food in my belly. I'm no one to judge what some of us have to endure....
Well, yes, fine. But what you're doing...you can't look at everything as a personal defeat.
...So I understand your talks with Eisenhower have more or less gone nowhere.
Yes, sir. The man won't acknowledge that there is any kind of problem. If he would just *open his mouth*, then things would happen.
I mean, as you know, he's refused to make a public defense of the Brown decision....

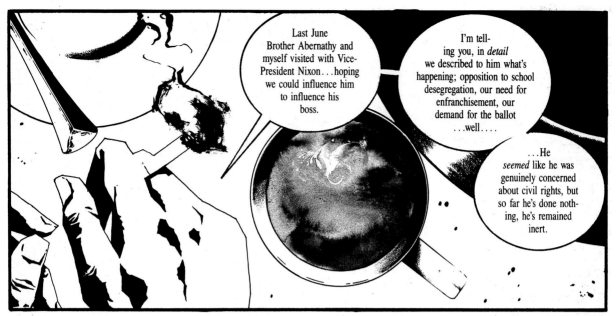

Last June Brother Abernathy and myself visited with Vice-President Nixon...hoping we could influence him to influence his boss.

I'm telling you, in *detail* we described to him what's happening; opposition to school desegregation, our need for enfranchisement, our demand for the ballot ...well....

...He *seemed* like he was genuinely concerned about civil rights, but so far he's done nothing, he's remained inert.

King, you should give Nixon a chance. I think he a lovely man. He h charm about him, seems legitimately concerned....

I actually... I recently heard that on Capitol Hill, Senator Johnson, the Texas senator, herded a civil rights bill through the Senate —

Yes, sir, Mr. Randolph, but in doing so, he bartered away any injunctive power the Attorney General might have to enforce school desegregation.

What the hell was Johnson thinking?

Just because it's the first civil rights legislation since Reconstruction, I think that he —

No, we're *very* unhappy with it —

Yes. Frankly, I agree with you, Martin. This bill all but ignores the school problem and voting rights.

And the Justice Department has enforced what little is good about it with all deliberate lethargy —

Well, that's what I'm talking about. This is where the SCLC comes in.

LAYING TONITE
BIRD

Bayard Rustin and myself called together, I think it was something like 115 Negro leaders to Montgomery to plan a counteroffensive, predominantly church leaders.

Now, Mr. Wilkins, please don't take offense at this, I know you can get defensive sometimes — unlike the NAACP, which is a membership organization, we've planned SCLC to consist of local affiliates, we think this will be a more effective strategy.

Basically, what we want is to operate through the churches and function as a service agency to coordinate local civil rights activity by means of bi-annual conventions with delegates of the various affiliates.

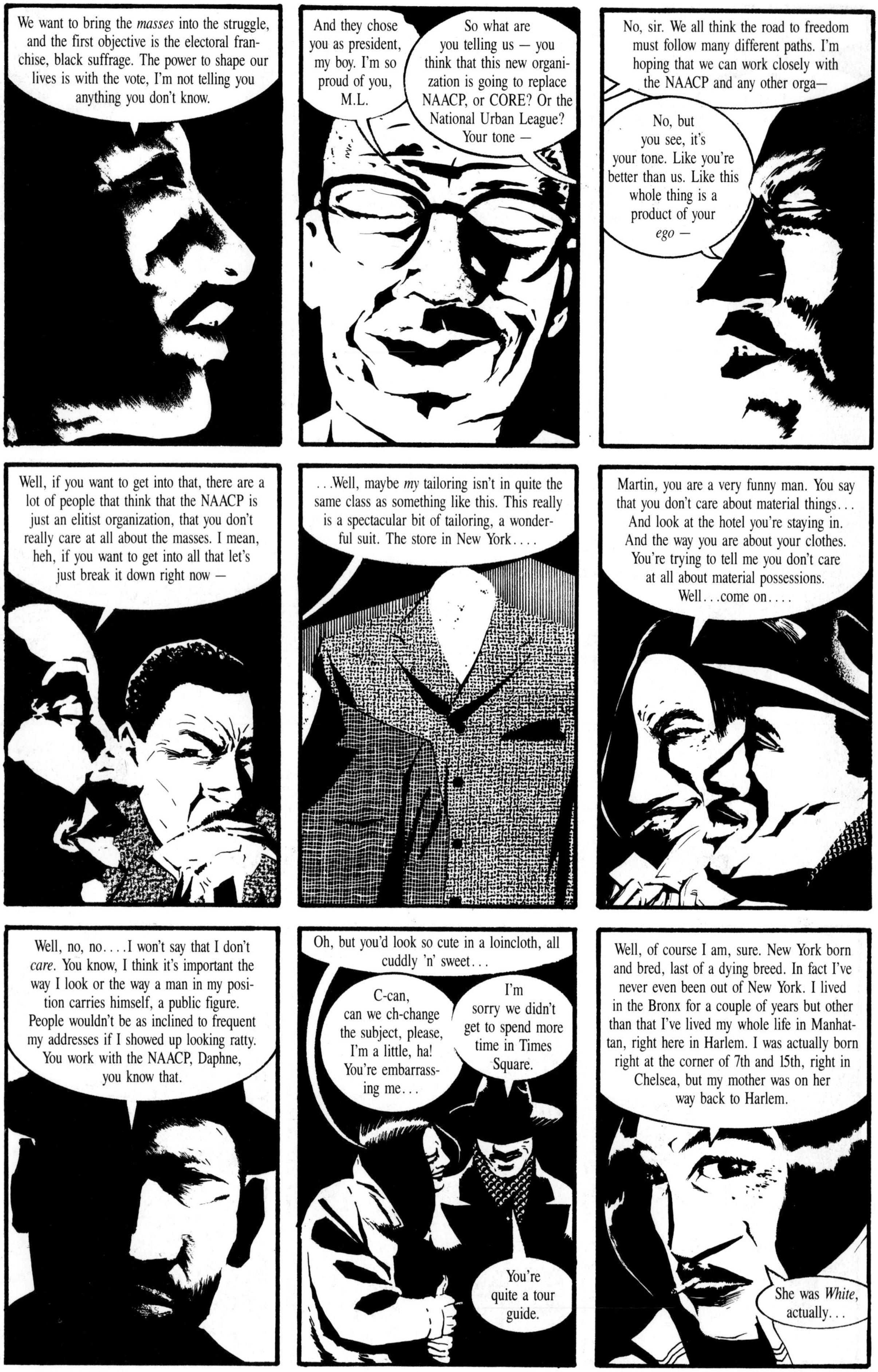
We want to bring the *masses* into the struggle, and the first objective is the electoral franchise, black suffrage. The power to shape our lives is with the vote, I'm not telling you anything you don't know.
And they chose you as president, my boy. I'm so proud of you, M.L.
So what are you telling us — you think that this new organization is going to replace NAACP, or CORE? Or the National Urban League? Your tone —
No, sir. We all think the road to freedom must follow many different paths. I'm hoping that we can work closely with the NAACP and any other orga—
No, but you see, it's your tone. Like you're better than us. Like this whole thing is a product of your *ego* —
Well, if you want to get into that, there are a lot of people that think that the NAACP is just an elitist organization, that you don't really care at all about the masses. I mean, heh, if you want to get into all that let's just break it down right now —
...Well, maybe *my* tailoring isn't in quite the same class as something like this. This really is a spectacular bit of tailoring, a wonderful suit. The store in New York....
Martin, you are a very funny man. You say that you don't care about material things... And look at the hotel you're staying in. And the way you are about your clothes. You're trying to tell me you don't care at all about material possessions. Well...come on....
Well, no, no....I won't say that I don't *care*. You know, I think it's important the way I look or the way a man in my position carries himself, a public figure. People wouldn't be as inclined to frequent my addresses if I showed up looking ratty. You work with the NAACP, Daphne, you know that.
Oh, but you'd look so cute in a loincloth, all cuddly 'n' sweet...
C-can, can we ch-change the subject, please, I'm a little, ha! You're embarrassing me...
I'm sorry we didn't get to spend more time in Times Square.
You're quite a tour guide.
Well, of course I am, sure. New York born and bred, last of a dying breed. In fact I've never even been out of New York. I lived in the Bronx for a couple of years but other than that I've lived my whole life in Manhattan, right here in Harlem. I was actually born right at the corner of 7th and 15th, right in Chelsea, but my mother was on her way back to Harlem.
She was *White*, actually...

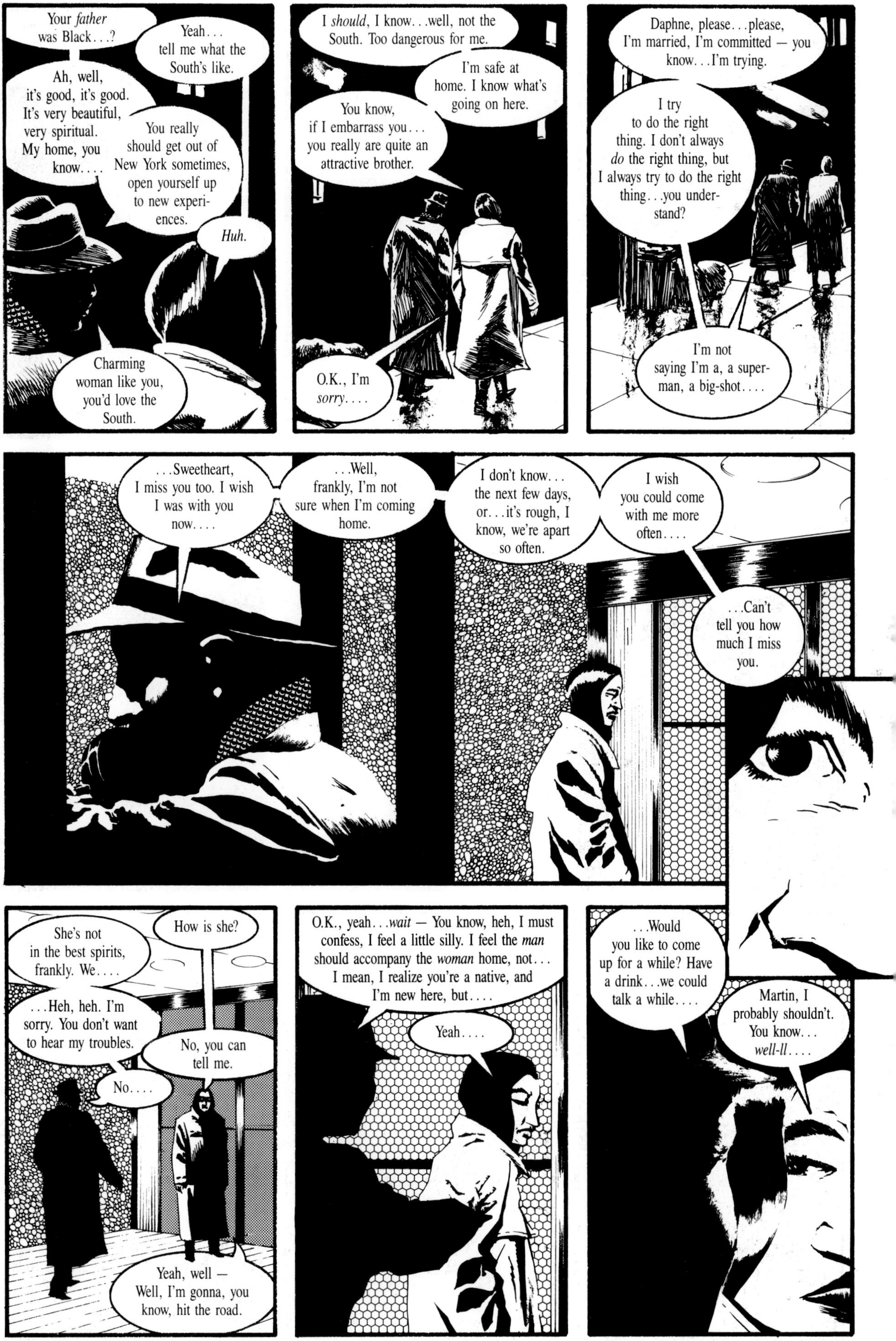
Your *father* was Black. . .?
Yeah. . . tell me what the South's like.
Ah, well, it's good, it's good. It's very beautiful, very spiritual. My home, you know. . . .
You really should get out of New York sometimes, open yourself up to new experi-ences.
Huh.
Charming woman like you, you'd love the South.
I *should*, I know. . .well, not the South. Too dangerous for me.
I'm safe at home. I know what's going on here.
You know, if I embarrass you. . . you really are quite an attractive brother.
O.K., I'm *sorry*. . . .
Daphne, please. . .please, I'm married, I'm committed — you know. . .I'm trying.
I try to do the right thing. I don't always *do* the right thing, but I always try to do the right thing. . .you under-stand?
I'm not saying I'm a, a super-man, a big-shot. . . .
. . .Sweetheart, I miss you too. I wish I was with you now. . . .
. . .Well, frankly, I'm not sure when I'm coming home.
I don't know. . . the next few days, or. . .it's rough, I know, we're apart so often.
I wish you could come with me more often. . . .
. . .Can't tell you how much I miss you.
She's not in the best spirits, frankly. We. . . .
How is she?
. . .Heh, heh. I'm sorry. You don't want to hear my troubles.
No, you can tell me.
No. . . .
Yeah, well — Well, I'm gonna, you know, hit the road.
O.K., yeah. . .*wait* — You know, heh, I must confess, I feel a little silly. I feel the *man* should accompany the *woman* home, not. . . I mean, I realize you're a native, and I'm new here, but. . . .
Yeah. . . .
. . .Would you like to come up for a while? Have a drink. . .we could talk a while. . . .
Martin, I probably shouldn't. You know. . . *well-ll*. . . .

The first thing the *Southern Christian Leadership Conference* decided upon doing came to be known as the Crusade for Citizen, a Southern-wide voter drive designed to double the number of Black voters by 1960, a voting year, to demonstrate that —

— *A new negro determined to be free had emerged in America.*

Those were his words. If the South's five million eligible Black voters could gain the ballot, and at the time only 1.3 million enjoyed this fundamental American right —

— King envisioned a solid block of 10 million voters across the U.S., who could wield formidable political power in the forthcoming election.

Voting clinics were set up all across Dixie conducted by the SCLC, to gather evidence of White obstructionism, train youths and adult leaders in nonviolence, and utilize the media to educate White Americans on the plight of Southern Blacks.

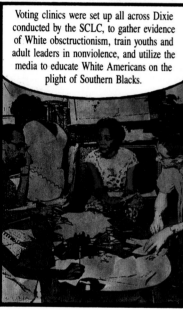

A central office was set up in Atlanta, and mainly through donations an operating fund of $250,000 was established. King hoped the campaign would attract the support of the Civil Rights Commission, the Senate... and Southern White moderates.

But of course there were problems. A lot of people, like Ella Baker, felt the whole SCLC project was a product of Dr. King's ego, that it all centered around him, which may or may not have been true. Personally... I think it was.

The crusade started on Lincoln's birthday in 1958, with a series of mass meetings taking place simultaneously all across Dixie.

Let us make our intentions crystal clear. We must and we will be free. We want freedom NOW.

We want the right to vote NOW. We do not want freedom fed to us in teaspoons over another 150 years. Under God we were born free. Misguided men robbed us of our freedom. We want it back.

Basically, the meetings were a rallying cry for Blacks to get off dey butts and go out and demand to use the right that was given to them a hundred years previous. The right to play a hand in shaping their own lives. The right to vote.

When we Blacks tried to vote...more often than not there was violence.

Whooa, whoa, whoa — Where d'ya think you're going, motherfucker? Hey, whoa —

— I asked you a question, where you going?

To vote, I'm going to vo—

The fuck you are, nigger.

Heh, you hear that, Charlie? —

Eventually SCLC resolved to file voter-registration complaints with the CRC.

SCLC strongly supported its recommendation that federal registrars be deployed in Southern areas where Blacks were systematically kept off the voting rolls and out of politics.

February 2, 1960

Four North Carolina A&T college students marched into a Woolworths and sat down at its lunch counter demanding to be served. This started the student sit-ins. Galvanized by their courage, soon hundreds of students were doing the same all over the South.

This was another form of protest to force desegregation. King was delighted that finally students were getting up and doing something to make their lives better, becoming involved in the struggle.

WE WANT TO SIT DOWN LIKE ANYONE ELSE

On the 13th of the month the largest sit-in was staged when 500 students crowded into White lunch counters in Nashville. King urged the students to follow the "Montgomery way," to not shove back when Whites shoved them and screamed at them.

In the eyes of the Lord, who looks worse, the oppressed or the oppressor? In March students held a demonstration at the county courthouse in Alabama.

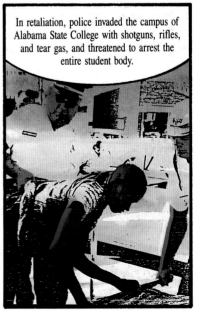

In retaliation, police invaded the campus of Alabama State College with shotguns, rifles, and tear gas, and threatened to arrest the entire student body.

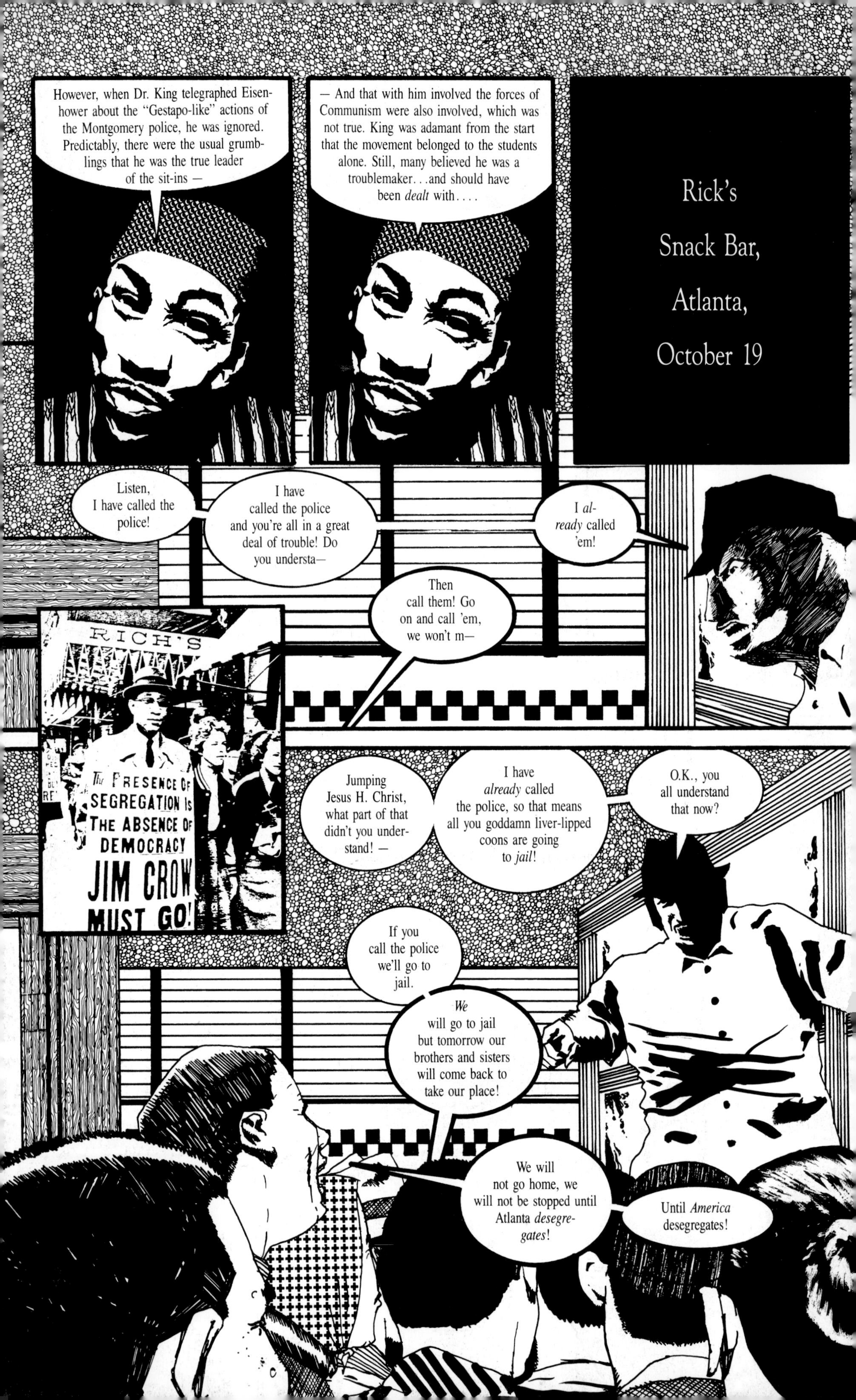
However, when Dr. King telegraphed Eisenhower about the "Gestapo-like" actions of the Montgomery police, he was ignored. Predictably, there were the usual grumblings that he was the true leader of the sit-ins —
— And that with him involved the forces of Communism were also involved, which was not true. King was adamant from the start that the movement belonged to the students alone. Still, many believed he was a troublemaker. . .and should have been *dealt* with. . . .
Rick's Snack Bar, Atlanta, October 19
Listen, I have called the police!
I have called the police and you're all in a great deal of trouble! Do you understa—
I *al-ready* called 'em!
Then call them! Go on and call 'em, we won't m—
RICH'S
The PRESENCE OF SEGREGATION IS THE ABSENCE OF DEMOCRACY JIM CROW MUST GO!
Jumping Jesus H. Christ, what part of that didn't you under-stand! —
I have *already* called the police, so that means all you goddamn liver-lipped coons are going to *jail*!
O.K., you all understand that now?
If you call the police we'll go to jail.
We will go to jail but tomorrow our brothers and sisters will come back to take our place!
We will not go home, we will not be stopped until Atlanta *desegregates*!
Until *America* desegregates!

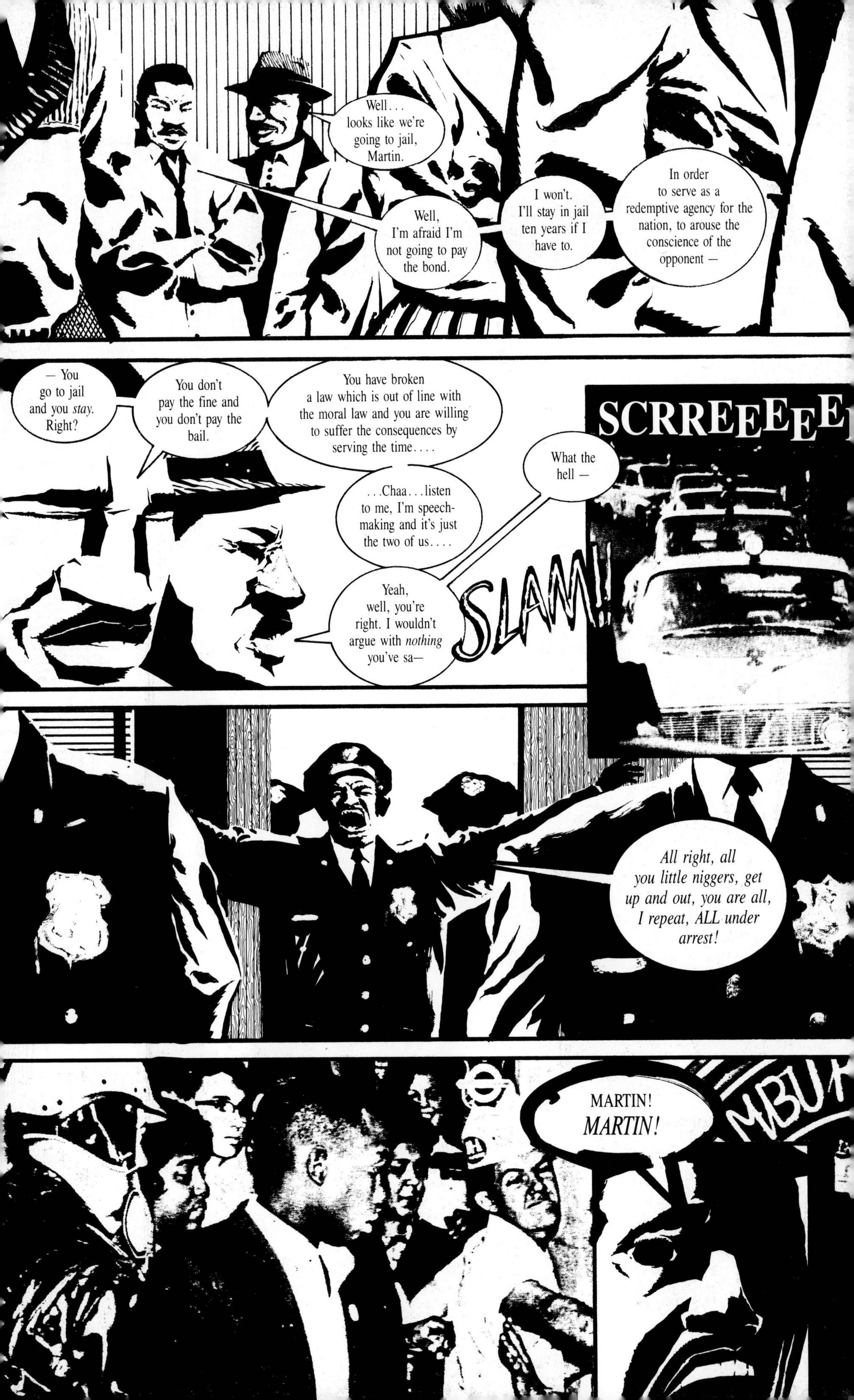

Well . . . looks like we're going to jail, Martin.
Well, I'm afraid I'm not going to pay the bond.
I won't. I'll stay in jail ten years if I have to.
In order to serve as a redemptive agency for the nation, to arouse the conscience of the opponent —
— You go to jail and you *stay*. Right?
You don't pay the fine and you don't pay the bail.
You have broken a law which is out of line with the moral law and you are willing to suffer the consequences by serving the time. . . .
. . . Chaa . . . listen to me, I'm speech-making and it's just the two of us. . . .
Yeah, well, you're right. I wouldn't argue with *nothing* you've sa—
SLAM!
What the hell —
SCRREEEEE
All right, all you little niggers, get up and out, you are all, I repeat, ALL under arrest!
MARTIN! *MARTIN!*

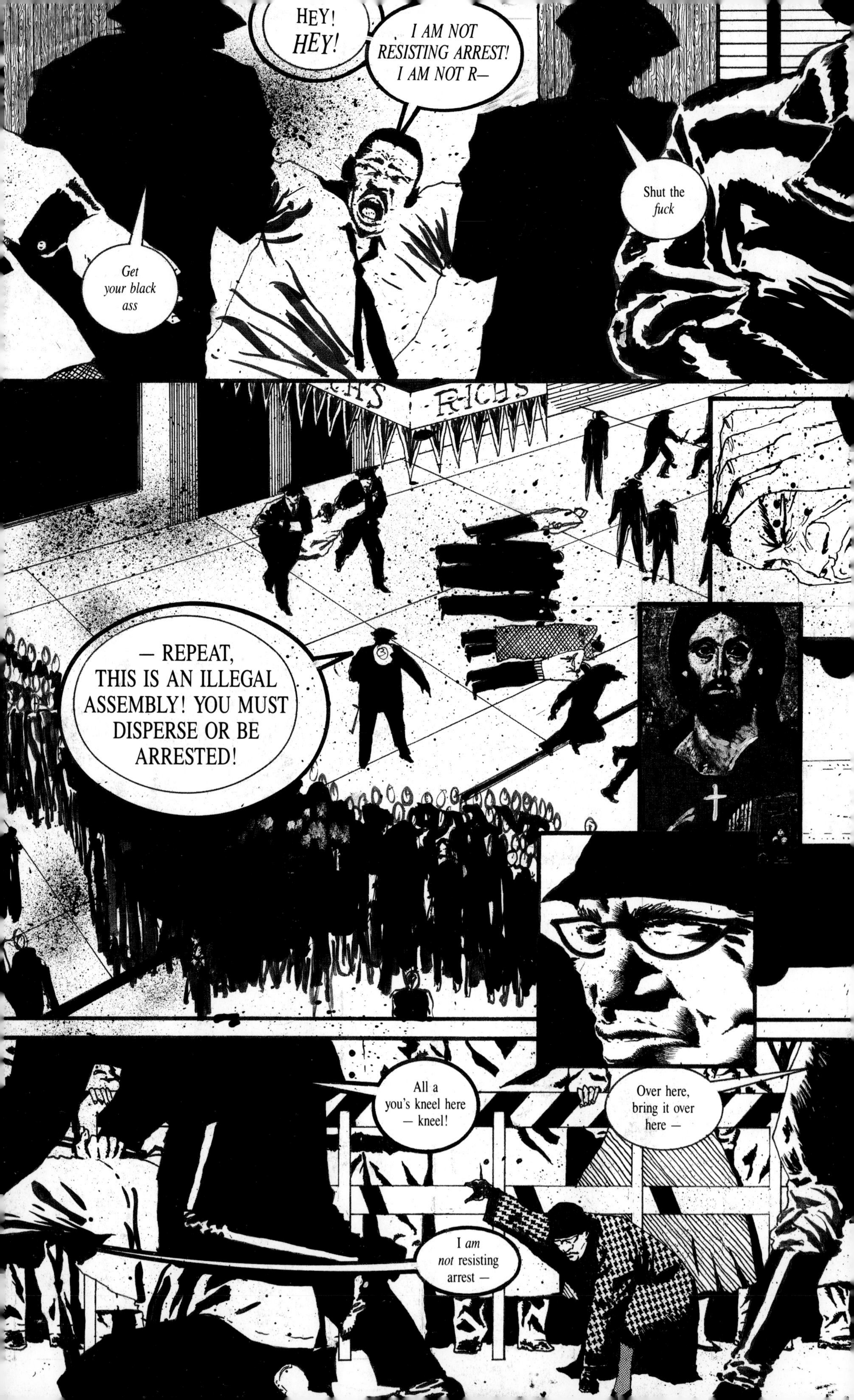
HEY! HEY!
I AM NOT RESISTING ARREST! I AM NOT R—
Get your black ass
Shut the *fuck*
— REPEAT, THIS IS AN ILLEGAL ASSEMBLY! YOU MUST DISPERSE OR BE ARRESTED!
All a you's kneel here — kneel!
Over here, bring it over here —
I *am* *not* resisting arrest —